THE HABITATION SOCIETY

"Fred Block offers a timely and thought-provoking perspective that challenges the conventional economic thinking on consumption, production, innovation and investment. He provides a compelling roadmap for moving towards a habitation society where individuals have greater agency in shaping their environments and communities. Recognizing that the economy does not only have a rate but a direction, Block illuminates opportunities for meaningful change towards shared goals. *The Habitation Society* is essential reading for anyone seeking to understand the ills of our contemporary economic system and envision a more just and sustainable future."
Mariana Mazzucato, author of *Mission Economy: A Moonshot Guide to Changing Capitalism*

"An impressive project for a democratic, postindustrial as well as postcapitalist political economy taking advantage of the crisis of capitalist globalization. The book develops the contours of a progressive model of prosperity, centred on the living conditions of ordinary people and based on collaborative production and investment by public agencies and private households integrated in networked communities. A blueprint, ambitious and optimistic, for an economy opting out of the logic of profit-making in favour of a logic of people-serving, moving from hierarchy to cooperation in democratic organizational forms."
Wolfgang Streeck, Max Planck Institute for the Study of Societies, Cologne

"The US economy is mostly a mess and most economists are making it worse. Fred Block explains why, combining sociological insights with practical suggestions for change. His take-down of conventional measures of investment should both embarrass Wall Street and inspire advocates for greater public spending on human and social capabilities."
Nancy Folbre, Professor Emerita of Economics, University of Massachusetts Amherst

"In *The Habitation Society*, Block offers a compelling critique of our current economic problems and a visionary sketch of a more democratic mode of governing the infrastructure of everyday life, through which we can create a more innovative, habitable and just society. This is a must-read for everyone interested in reviving democracy and reimagining an economy that works for everyone."
Elizabeth Anderson, Max Shaye Professor of Public Philosophy, Uni

"In this brilliant new work, Fred Block compels us to rethink our long-held assumptions about economy and society. Economic gurus describe an industrial economy that no longer exists, blind to the new 'habitation economy' built on our collective social infrastructure – from public investments to familial care. Above all, the book warns us of the urgency to democratize financialization and accelerate citizenship participation if we are to thwart authoritarianism and instead create an equitable habitation society."

Margaret R. Somers, Professor Emerita of Sociology and History, University of Michigan, Ann Abor

"This is an exciting book on how to improve human flourishing by creating, maintaining, and improving the socioeconomic and biophysical infrastructures of local communities that cannot be bought and sold like standardized commodities. Fred Block illustrates how neoliberal globalization undermined mutual recognition and norms of reciprocity, showing at the same time the potential of democratizing habitation by satisfying needs for housing, energy, care, and food, while also creating a habitat for plants, animals, and other life forms."

Andreas Novy, WU Vienna University of Economics, President, International Karl Polanyi Society

"*The Habitation Society* is a Copernican shift to a new paradigm for understanding the profound economic, political and social changes of our moment. Deeply anchored in the larger context of the past 200 years, Fred Block's vision of 'the habitation society' offers convincing and compelling links between past political economies and future possibilities. Its reader-friendly pages offer a much-needed field guide for building bridges to a better world."

Kathryn Kish Sklar, Distinguished Professor Emerita, State University of New York at Binghamton

"*The Habitation Society* is a succinct, cogent argument for restructuring economic priorities and reconstructing democratic governance. By rethinking conventional economic wisdom and providing strategies for delivering the physical and social infrastructure communities need, Block lays out a way forward. Everyone who cares about the future, activists and theorists alike, should dig into this book."

Peter Evans, Professor Emeritus, Department of Sociology, University of California, Berkeley

BUILDING PROGRESSIVE ALTERNATIVES

Series Editors: David Coates†, Ben Rosamond and Matthew Watson

Bringing together economists, political economists and other social scientists, this series offers pathways to a coherent, credible and progressive economic growth strategy which, when accompanied by an associated set of wider public policies, can inspire and underpin the revival of a successful centre-left politics in advanced capitalist societies.

Published

Corbynism in Perspective: The Labour Party under Jeremy Corbyn
Edited by Andrew S. Roe-Crines

Divided They Fell: Crisis and the Collapse of Europe's Centre-Left
Sean McDaniel

Europe and the British Left: Beyond the Progressive Dilemma
Owen Parker, Matthew Louis Bishop and Nicole Lindstrom

The European Social Question: Tackling Key Controversies
Amandine Crespy

Flawed Capitalism: The Anglo-American Condition and its Resolution
David Coates

Getting Over New Labour: The Party After Blair and Brown
Karl Pike

The Habitation Society: Creating Sustainable Prosperity
Fred Block

The Political Economy of Industrial Strategy in the UK: From Productivity Problems to Development Dilemmas
Edited by Craig Berry, Julie Froud and Tom Barker

Pursuing the Knowledge Economy: A Sympathetic History of High-Skill, High-Wage Hubris
Nick O'Donovan

Race and the Undeserving Poor: From Abolition to Brexit
Robbie Shilliam

Reflections on the Future of the Left
Edited by David Coates

THE HABITATION SOCIETY

Creating Sustainable Prosperity

Fred Block

agenda
publishing

For my grandchildren: Devorah, Elio, and Gabriel

© Fred Block 2025

This book is copyright under the Berne Convention.
No reproduction without permission.
All rights reserved.

First published in 2025 by Agenda Publishing

Agenda Publishing Limited
PO Box 185
Newcastle upon Tyne
NE20 2DH

www.agendapub.com

ISBN 978-1-78821-749-1 (hardcover)
ISBN 978-1-78821-750-7 (paperback)

British Library Cataloguing-in-Publication Data
A catalogue record for this book is available
from the British Library

Typeset in Nocturne by Patty Rennie

Printed and bound in the UK by
CPI Group (UK) Ltd, Croydon, CR0 4YY

Contents

	Preface	ix
1.	Accounting for morbid symptoms	1
2.	Why habitation?	21
3.	Commodification without the commodities	47
4.	The irony of corporate dominance	65
5.	What counts as investment?	91
6.	Dysfunctional financing	119
7.	Democratizing habitation	137
	Notes	161
	References	169
	Index	179

Preface

This book has a very long history. My politics and my worldview were a product of a time very long ago—the 1960s. I was part of the New Left in the U.S. as an undergraduate (1964–68) and as a graduate student (1968–74). My values and my understanding of politics were shaped by a movement that struggled for racial justice, to stop the Vietnam War, and to challenge corporate power. But while my core convictions have not changed, reality today is in many ways different from what it was in the 1960s. I have attempted to develop new language and new concepts to make my old values relevant to the lived experience of the third decade of the twenty-first century.

In the student movement of the 1960s, we believed in something called "participatory democracy"—the idea that people should have much greater influence over decisions shaping their lives than was possible through voting in periodic elections. While our youthful dreams of radical change were not realized as the United States moved steadily rightward in subsequent decades, I have held on to that vision of a society in which ordinary people were empowered. This book is an effort to give that idea of participatory democracy new relevance and new urgency.

With ideas that have gestated over 60 years, I have accumulated more intellectual debts that I can possibly acknowledge here. First and foremost, there is a group of friends and close colleagues who have sustained me over many decades of continuous conversations and debates. This group includes Peter Evans, Larry Hirschhorn, Carole Joffe, Karl

Klare, Magali Sarfatti Larson, Marguerite Mendell, Frances Fox Piven, Michael Reich, Margaret Somers, Howard Winant, and the late Erik Olin Wright. Matthew R. Keller and Marian Negoita have worked with me for almost 20 years exploring the complexities of government-sponsored innovation in the U.S. and other nations. My co-editor for *Democratizing Finance*, Robert Hockett helped to deepen my understanding of finance and credit.

I amassed a huge debt to faculty colleagues and graduate students in the Sociology Department at the University of California, Davis. I have served on the editorial board of *Politics & Society* since 1978, and have learned a huge amount from reading manuscripts and discussing with fellow board members. The section on Economic Sociology in the American Sociological Association has also played a critical role in my development. There are simply too many valued colleagues to enumerate. I have also benefited from years of participation in a political economy and history reading group organized by Kathryn Sklar and Thomas Dublin. Since 2014, I have worked to create the Center for Engaged Scholarship, and I have incurred a deep debt to my co-conspirator Mridula Udayagiri and to the many faculty and fellows who have participated in a series of stimulating dissertation workshops. I am also deeply grateful to the political economy reading group at the University of Michigan that read a draft of the book.

Alison Howson, my editor at Agenda is due special thanks. She was the one who first suggested that the habitation concept was worthy of a book, and it was her gentle prodding that got me to do this. Carole Joffe and our daughters have sustained me through many decades of challenges, disappointments, and epiphanies. The debt I owe them is beyond words.

An earlier version of Chapter 3 was published as "Beyond the Commodity: Toward a New Understanding of Economic Modernity" in *American Affairs* 4:3 (2020). I am grateful to the Economy and Society program at the Hewlett Foundation for supporting that project and for those who provided feedback on that paper. A version of Chapter 5 was published as "What Counts as Investment: Productive and Unproductive Expenditures" in *Theory and Society* 53 (2024).

1

Accounting for morbid symptoms

"The crisis consists precisely in the fact that the old is dying and the new cannot be born; in this interregnum a great variety of morbid symptoms appear."
Antonio Gramsci, *Prison Notebooks*, 1930.[1]

The quote from Antonio Gramsci's *Prison Notebooks* from 1930 is eerily relevant to our current historical moment. The morbid symptoms that he had in mind included Mussolini's fascist regime that had imprisoned him and the growing strength of Hitler's National Socialist Party in Germany. Today's morbid symptoms are the rising threats to democratic governance posed by ultranationalist right-wing movements and leaders. Using the fascist label for Vladimir Putin, Victor Orbán, Jair Bolsonaro, and Donald Trump remains controversial partly because these leaders have not yet assembled paramilitary gangs dressed in uniforms of the same color. Nevertheless, their unrelenting hostility to liberal democratic norms and institutions is beyond debate.

But why is democratic governance now experiencing the most intense challenges since the 1930s? One powerful explanation emphasizes the global reign of neoliberal or market fundamentalist economic ideas from the late 1970s down to the current moment.[2] Those ideas have led to reduced taxation of corporations and the very wealthy, and constraints on the ability of governments to protect citizens from market fluctuations. Moreover, those ideas have changed the ground rules of the global economy in ways that further constrain what governments can provide to their own citizens. The result has been dramatic increases in income and wealth inequality and relatively slow growth of average household incomes. Frustrated voters have responded by turning to outsider candidates, sometimes of the far right, who promise to restore the good times of the past.

A compatible line of argument emphasizes political realignments that have come with rising educational levels in developed economies. Thomas Piketty has called this the "Brahminization of left parties."[3] Historically, the majority of voters with a college education had voted with right-wing parties, but in recent decades, much of this group has shifted their allegiance to parties of the left. This has diminished the focus of these parties on improving the economic situation of voters with lower levels of education. In the worst case, some left parties have embraced the neoliberal agenda that has further undermined the economic security of these voters with less education.[4] With their interests no longer being represented by the historic parties of the left, many of these voters have been attracted to the populist appeals of anti-liberal parties and movements.

However, neither of these explanations map on to the idea that Gramsci conveys by using the metaphor of childbirth. Gramsci is arguing that in the 1930s society needed to transition from one mode of economic and social organization to another, and yet this transition was not being allowed to happen. But in the development of societies, there is no equivalent to an emergency Caesarean to manage a dangerously delayed birth. In short, the morbid symptoms are equivalent to the possibility that both mother and baby will die as a result of a dangerously prolonged birthing experience.

Gramsci's morbid symptoms also evoke the confusion that comes from such a period of blocked transition. People are trying to make sense of what is going on within the categories of the old and dying social arrangements, but those ideas are completely inadequate for grasping the new reality. But since the transition has been stalled, there are not yet widely accepted concepts to make sense of what is happening. In short, another morbid symptom is the breakdown in rational debate as the political space is filled with conspiracy theories and disinformation.

Gramsci had been a leader of the Italian Communist Party, and he believed in 1930 that socialism was the new form of social organization whose birth was being blocked. His formulation was equivalent to that of other left theorists of the period who insisted that either society moves forward to socialism or backwards to the barbarism of fascism. However, with 90 years of additional historical knowledge, it seems that Gramsci's speculation was wrong. I would argue that the crisis of the interwar years that generated both the Great Depression and fascism was the result of society's inability to transition from a nineteenth-century model of capitalism to the kind of social democratic model that was broadly implemented after the Second World War. It was a mass consumption society that raised the living standards for both industrial workers and farmers that was struggling to be born in Gramsci's time.

There were some who clearly understood the transition that should be happening. Foremost among them was John Maynard Keynes who argued consistently from 1919 to his death in 1946 for a reform of capitalism in which the state would play an active role in assuring full employment by redistributing income downward and assuring high levels of public investment.[5] But Keynes was hardly alone; others also anticipated the emergence of a mass consumption society. Moreover, the policies pursued in the 1930s by Franklin Roosevelt's New Deal and the reforms of the Swedish Social Democratic Party demonstrated to other nations the possibility of this transition.

To make the quote from Gramsci relevant to our current predicament, we need to figure out what is the form of social organization whose birth is being blocked now. An answer emerges when we look squarely at the economic changes that have occurred over the last 50–60 years. Over this period, the number of employees who actually make tangible things—buildings, machinery, consumer products or agricultural goods—has dropped precipitously. In the U.S., for example, more than 80 per cent of people now work in the "service sector", an amorphous category whose main commonality is that the things produced are either intangible like financial services or transitory like a concert, restaurant meal, or a baseball game. Moreover, the number of people who spend part or all of their day working in front of some kind of computer screen has skyrocketed.[6]

For decades, analysts have argued that these are indications that we are shifting into a postindustrial society. However, the term "postindustrial" tells us nothing about this new form of social organization other than that it comes after industrialism. My argument is that we now have a "habitation" economy because most people work at creating, maintaining or improving the soft and hard infrastructure of the communities in which we live. The problem is that we do not yet have a habitation society since our economy continues to be organized through the structures, institutions, and concepts of an industrial economy. Even though most of us produce habitation and all of us consume habitation, we have been blocked from having the habitation that people actually want.

In brief, the old industrial economy is dying and the new habitation society cannot yet be born. Moreover, this incomplete transition is producing morbid symptoms that parallel those that Gramsci had in mind. Foremost among these is the crisis of democracy as many societies are threatened by right-wing authoritarians. But there is also the widespread confusion that Gramsci identified as the old categories of thought no longer work, but new understandings have not yet been adopted.

Specifically, it has become extremely difficult for people to understand their own relationship to the larger economy and society. Throughout history, most people could see the immediate consequences of their work effort when they dug a ditch, milked a cow, or produced a ceramic bowl. Even in a twentieth-century automotive factory, the number of hours worked on the assembly line translated into a certain number of cars that came off the line. Today, however, individual work has become either abstract or a part of a complex system where the consequences of individual effort are largely invisible. In factories, robots are performing many of the tasks that used to be done by humans. Activity by the remaining workers who oversee the automated systems is often intermittent, while demands on their attention are continuous and often extend beyond normal working hours. As a consequence, there is no longer an obvious relationship between the amount or intensity of work effort and economic output.

And yet, many work organizations continue to be obsessed with maximizing the output of each employee. New technologies provide real-time data to supervisors of the number of key strokes per hour of each employee or the amount of time that delivery trucks are not actually moving. Some physicians are required to limit each patient interaction to 15 minutes even if a longer session might be needed to get to the root of the patient's problem. But there is reason for skepticism that these efforts at controlling employees are actually increasing output.

Without a linear relationship between work time and output, it becomes much harder to understand how the individual fits into the larger economy. The vocalist, Tennessee Ernie Ford, sang about working in a mine to extract "16 tons" of coal each day. Instead of multiple tons of coal, today's workday for an average employee might consist of 20 emails, four memos, two Zoom calls with colleagues, six phone calls, three meetings, and a 30-minute repair on a piece of equipment. In short, how one's workday fits into the larger economy has become mysterious for many of us.

In the face of mysteries, people often resort to folk beliefs or superstitions to handle uncertainty. Some have responded to this more abstract and intangible economic reality by embracing a nineteenth-century imaginary of an economy made up of autonomous and independent workers, farmers, and artisans. Even when their work bears almost no resemblance to that historical reality, they still insist that their paycheck has been earned through the sweat of their own brow. Some of these people embrace an "everyday libertarianism" that argues that what is mine is mine and nobody else has a claim on it. It follows that they are resentful of the taxation system that insists on taking a share of that paycheck. They end up as believers in the magical power of the market to coordinate the labors of the many.[7]

Others, of course, have responded to the same circumstances in exactly the opposite way. Starting from intangible output and uncertain relation between work effort and work results, they conclude that the present highly unequal distribution of economic rewards is unjustified and that a more equal distribution of economic output is both feasible and just. In other words, an economy whose workings are mysterious generates radically divergent narratives about taxation, distribution, and redistribution. From such divergent beginnings, it is just a small step to intense and unbridgeable political disagreements.

ECONOMICS AND THE BLOCKED TRANSITION

Those who attribute the current crisis of democracy to decades of neoliberalism and parties of the left abandoning their working-class constituents are not wrong. It is just that they also need to recognize that the neoliberal turn in policy was an expedient designed to block the transition to a different type of society. As early as the 1960s, a number of writers, led by Daniel Bell, argued that the shift to a service economy and the increased use of computers was driving fundamental social changes.[8] Realizing the potential of this new postindustrial society required a significant shift in the relationship between business and the state. The role of government had to expand as the division of labor became more complex and more dependent on technological advances.

However, the free-market economist Milton Friedman and his allies argued exactly the opposite. They insisted that as the division of labor became ever more complex, the only way to make the economy work effectively was to *reduce* the role of government. By relying more on markets and less on government, any economic problems could be solved. This position was attractive to much of the business community that was already feeling threatened by increases in government regulatory initiatives. In short, enthusiastic support from business allowed the free-market position to win the political battle despite the inherent implausibility of the claim that reliance on markets would make an ever more complex economy function effectively.

This rise of neoliberalism was also critically enabled by the discipline of economics. While many economists were skeptical of Friedman's extreme conservative views, the discipline has a core belief that helped give neoliberal ideas far more plausibility than they deserved. Most economists insist that their basic tools and analyses are valuable regardless of whether an economy is producing agricultural goods, manufactured goods, or services. In this view, economics is about optimizing the use of inputs—capital investment, labor, raw materials, and energy—to produce any set of outputs. An economist who served as a U.S. presidential economic advisor is alleged to have quipped: "Potato chips, computer chips, what's the difference? A hundred dollars of one or a hundred dollars of the other is still a hundred dollars." Underlying the remark is a shared belief among economists that changes over time in what an economy produces and how it is produced are largely irrelevant. Most economic output has a specific monetary value, and economics is about maximizing the efficiency with which inputs are transformed into outputs that are aggregated into measures such as gross domestic product (GDP).

With this justification, mainstream economists have made only minor adjustments to their theoretical framework despite the dramatic changes in the economy over the last six decades. New ideas emerge among economists all the time, and some of them become widely disseminated. However, it is still the consensus view that changes over the past 60 years do not quire a serious reconsideration of earlier assumptions about what is or is not economically productive. It is this feature of the discipline that allowed its prestige and influence to be captured and weaponized by market fundamentalists who made consistently extreme and implausible claims about the power of markets to coordinate economic activity.

WHAT THIS BOOK OFFERS

This book, in contrast, begins its analysis with the economy as it actually exists in the present and seeks to map out what would make that economy work more effectively. The goal is to demystify the economy, so that it becomes easier for people to understand how their activity fits into the larger economic fabric. The hope is to empower individuals to recognize the kinds of changes that could be made to the economy that would improve things for themselves, their families, their neighbors, and their communities. This necessarily requires a conversation with mainstream economic arguments, showing where they are mistaken given how much has changed in the economy. Hopefully, I can also persuade mainstream economists that it is time to abandon the mistaken view that it does not matter whether the economy is making potato chips or computer chips.

The book also has another goal. Ever since the rise of modern industry in the early nineteenth century, there has been a dream that the fantastic productivity of factory production could usher in a society without vast inequalities of income and wealth and political power. The British industrialist, Robert Owen, created a model textile factory at New Lanark in Scotland in the first decades of the nineteenth century, and he was one of the first to articulate this dream. However, 200 years of agitation by socialists and other radicals have failed to make the dream a reality. Communist regimes in places such as Cuba and China have been successful in raising living standards for the poor, but they have failed in equalizing the distribution of wealth and political power. Scandinavian societies also made great progress in the second half of the twentieth century in reducing inequality between the middle class and the working class, but since then they seem to have regressed towards greater inequality.

In short, the path to a more egalitarian and more democratic society has effectively been blocked. A global billionaire class has grown both in numbers and in political power and in many places has become entangled with authoritarian leaders and far-right social movements. In place after place, the alliance of oligarchs and right-wing movements threatens the survival of democratic institutions. Moreover, financialization in the global economy means that speculators can initiate runs on the bonds and the currencies of governments that initiate unorthodox economic policies. This provides an effective constraint on political leaders who might otherwise be tempted to pursue more egalitarian and more inclusive policies.

Nevertheless, I am arguing that there is now a feasible pathway for significant egalitarian transformation of existing developed economies. It is not a simple path and there are no guarantees that pursuing it will be effective or successful. Yet the book seeks to illuminate these opportunities for social movements that have the vision and organizational capacity to build majoritarian political coalitions.

The argument of the book is most relevant to the world's developed market economies, especially the 38 nations that are part of the Organization of Economic Cooperation and Development (OECD). The OECD reports that service sector employment accounts for 70 per cent of employment for its member countries. These are the nations that are nearest to a transition to a habitation society. However, the argument also has considerable relevance to a number of middle-income nations, including China, as they think through their development plans. There are potential "advantages of backwardness" since it is possible for nations to leap ahead by avoiding some of the most wasteful policies associated with mass consumption economies.

However, most of the examples used and much of the data are drawn from the United States. This is because the United States is the case that I know the best, and it would take too much time to add examples and data from additional countries. However, the U.S. has been a world leader in creating a mass consumption economy, and there are many features of U.S. development that have been emulated by other nations. Hence, the broad strokes of the analysis are relevant for many other societies even though there are significant differences across the developed market economies around the organization of healthcare, higher education, housing markets, and other areas of consumption. I would also suggest that while some nations have moved somewhat closer to creating a habitation society than the United States, no nation has yet completed this transition.

The following sections offer brief summaries of the key themes and arguments presented in the book's six chapters.

HABITATION

The foundation of the argument is that we need to transition from an industrial society to a habitation society. Habitation is the process of creating, maintaining, and improving the social and physical infrastructure of human communities. People have always needed to construct and maintain habitation. Even nomadic peoples still build temporary habitation as they wander from site to site. But during the industrial era, habitation work was done in the background; it happened when people were finished with the primary tasks of work on farms or in factories.

In our current service economy, however, the largest category of employment is habitation work. As the share of the labor force producing food or manufactured goods has declined, most employment focuses on the social and physical infrastructure of our communities. This includes construction work, education, childcare, healthcare, communications, transportation, energy, entertainment, local government, and the expanding labor force that works on research and development as part of the innovation economy.

Moreover, while most people work, either paid or unpaid, in producing habitation, almost all of us consume habitation. The sole exceptions are a few hermits living in remote locations. But even though most of us produce and also consume habitation, we have relatively little voice in shaping that habitation. So, for example, it is the exception rather than the rule that decisions about infrastructure such as the location of highways, mass transit, high-speed rail lines, airports, or even parks are made through some kind of inclusive public deliberation. People also lack much influence over a critical part of habitation: the location and availability of affordable housing.

Moreover, almost all of the communities in which we live have been shaped or misshaped to one degree or another by two powerful and destructive patterns. First, the histories of racial and ethnic hierarchies have structured the geographies of our living spaces. The dispossession of Indigenous peoples, the legacy of slavery, the aftermath of colonization, and the uneven incorporation of different waves of immigration have left their mark on our settlements. This is visible in small towns where the railroad tracks separate the middle class from the poor and in metropolises that are carved up into multiple neighborhoods characterized by differing levels of privilege and neglect.

Second, our settlements are the products of many decades of misguided policies that assumed that nature could be dominated and subdued if only we used enough concrete and asphalt. Habitations were constructed around abundant and cheap fossil fuels. But with rising temperatures, more extreme weather, floods, wildfires, and environmental contamination, the need to reverse these earlier mistakes is increasingly obvious. Moreover, these histories intersect, so that the neighborhoods where many historically marginalized people live are also those facing the most extreme environmental challenges.

However, the ability of people to respond and remedy these historical legacies is limited because of the absence of effective democratic control over key habitation decisions. This lack of democratic control also has deep historical roots. In the industrial era, questions of urban infrastructure and development were deliberately removed from political debate with authority handed over to technocratic experts. The enormous influence of Robert Moses on the development of the New York metropolitan area through his leadership of several public works and planning agencies that were insulated from public input is a paradigmatic example of this history. Moreover, cities and towns are usually unable to finance major infrastructure projects on their own either through tax revenue or borrowing. Hence, the key decisions tend to be made at higher levels of government with significant input from financial interests who underwrite the bonds used to finance such expenditures. Without access to sufficient resources needed for reconstruction, local politics tends to generate into zero-sum fights among neighbors that often result in political paralysis.

At the same time, however, important contemporary social movements can be understood as efforts by people to exercise more control over their habitation. The obvious example are environmental movements including campaigns to achieve environmental justice. There is also increasing activism against homelessness, high rents, and for increased availability of affordable housing. Movements for racial justice and to halt racist policing and to end mass incarceration are also efforts by communities to exert more influence on their habitation. There are also significant grassroots efforts to reform the healthcare system and the education system to make them less bureaucratic, more inclusive, and more able to respond to community needs. There is also increasing mobilization to increase the availability and quality of care including childcare, mental health care, and care for older people.

The argument is that these various movements could be more powerful and more effective by recognizing themselves as engaged in the shared project of democratizing habitation. Such a project would have two central foci. The first would be expanding the financial resources available to localities, so that citizens would have enough funds to negotiate positive-sum solutions to pressing problems. The second would be to expand citizen input into decision making. If, for example, communities worked to increase environmental resilience while also expanding the availability of affordable housing, there would be the possibility of negotiating compromises that began to address historical injustices while also improving the quality of life for most residents.

THE TRANSITION AWAY FROM CLASSICAL COMMODITIES

The emergence of a habitation economy entails an enormous shift in what it is that people consume. In the 1930s and 1940s, purchases of food and manufactured goods represented the bulk of what people consumed. Now, however, services, including housing, equal close to 80 per cent of what people purchase. This shift has dramatically reduced the role of standardized commodities in the economy. This is important because modern economics was built around the analysis of commodity production. All of those supply and demand curves are built on the premise that what people are buying are standardized goods, produced by multiple suppliers, that are transferred at a single moment in time.

These characteristics of traditional commodities made it possible for economists to establish the idea that markets were continuously brought into balance by the law of supply and demand. Since producers lacked market power and there were multiple suppliers, it was an easy matter for consumers to stop dealing with somebody who they thought to be charging too much. It was relatively costless to take one's business elsewhere.

However, when we think of what is consumed today, most items bear little resemblance to these traditional commodities. First, many of the services we consume—education, healthcare, financial services, restaurant meals—are supposed to be customized rather than standardized. Moreover, many of the goods that we consume come in such a wide variety of different types and styles that it is hard to pick out one or two examples that represent the whole class. Think of something as simple as a quart of milk. A generation ago, a quart of whole cow's milk represented most consumer milk purchases.[9] Now, however, demand is spread out across skim, 2%, whole, with reduced lactose, and then almond, oat, and a host of other nut and vegetable milks. Moreover, increasingly businesses are engaging in "mass customization" where they will produce an article of clothing, an automobile, a computer, or a piece of furniture that matches the specifications of each individual buyer.

Along with a decline in standardization comes a decline in the number of producers. Many of today's firms use protections on intellectual property such as patents and copyrights to make sure that they are the only business that produces a certain pharmaceutical, movie, television program, music recording, book, computer game, financial instrument, or software program. Many other markets are dominated by two, three, or four main providers who differentiate themselves more by product features than by pricing or terms of service. In the U.S., this increased level of concentration has been the result of the government largely abandoning antitrust enforcement between 1981 and 2020. With lax enforcement, concentration in industry after industry has risen substantially. The consequence is that a consumer can switch from one mobile phone company to another, but it is likely that the billing practices will be equally difficult to decipher.

Moreover, very few of these transactions occur at just one moment in time. Most purchases of services—education, healthcare, financial services, utilities—extend over a long period of time. This is also true of consumer durables such as automobiles, home appliances, heating and cooling equipment that increasingly involve service and maintenance contracts. In fact, more and more businesses are following an internet model of subscription services; the consumer does not just buy word-processing software or security software but instead subscribes to such services for a year at a time. However, when purchasing relationships extend over time, it means that the cost to consumers of switching providers increases substantially. There are often financial penalties for ending a contract early and a cost of time and energy.

In short, the decline of standardized commodities has dramatically increased the power of producers over consumers. We have been told repeatedly that a market economy is a magnificent instrument for allowing citizens to incentivize others to fulfill their needs, but this mechanism is no longer working. In the existing habitation economy, many people are not able to get the things they want from a market that has become increasingly unresponsive.

The corporate transition from vertical integration to collaborative network production

The shift away from standardized commodities is driving another critical change in the economy that undermines much of what is assumed in textbook economics. This is a shift in how many businesses go about production. The old days of mass production when firms would produce the same product year after year has disappeared. Today, most firms are constantly upgrading and changing the products that they bring to market. There is a huge emphasis on innovation, both in what is produced and how it is produced.

This shift means that most corporations need to partner with other organizations for both innovation and production. Sixty years ago, automotive companies did the bulk of the work in-house. Today, they rely on suppliers for 60–70 per cent of the value added of each vehicle. Moreover, with the transition to electric vehicles, they have to partner with both battery makers and firms with computer expertise to launch new models.

This shift is most dramatic with the innovation process. Most large firms have significantly reduced the size of their own corporate laboratory or actually closed it, and they increasingly rely on collaborations with other firms and with publicly-funded institutes to develop new products and new processes. What is driving this process is the increasing importance of highly specialized expertise, the kind that is acquired only after years and years of engagement with a specific set of problems. It is the type of expertise that research scientists have and that skilled craftspeople acquired over years of apprenticeship.

In their day-to-day operations, vertically organized firms managed by reducing their dependence on that kind of specialized expertise. Automotive firms, for example, systematically replaced craftworkers with semi-skilled assembly-line workers who could learn their jobs in a few weeks. Now, however, as specialized expertise becomes more essential, we are seeing a transition from vertical integration to collaborative network production.

In a system of collaborative network production, the importance of small and medium-sized firms increases since they are often the most attractive employers for people with these specialized types of expertise. At the same time, the economic role of government also increases for two reasons. First, the government creates and funds public research centers that foster innovation. Second, governmental actors play a critical role in facilitating and supporting the network ties that are critical for collaborative network production.

The problem, however, is that a full transition to collaborative network production has been blocked by the institutional power of existing large corporations. They have been able to use both market power and their political clout to defend their entrenched positions and hold on to a disproportionate share of the profits generated by the production process.

THE TRANSFORMATION OF INVESTMENT

One of the central errors that stands in the way of democratizing habitation is the mismeasurement of investment. Investment is one of the central categories of economics. It is generally defined as outlays to pay for goods that will make possible the production of other goods. If I have a shop that sells bagels, and I buy a new oven that increases my bagel-making capacity, that counts as an investment. In conventional economic accounting, output is divided into three buckets. In the first bucket are all of the things that we consume in a given time period. Second are investment expenditures, and third are intermediate goods that are used up in the process of production such as the metal, glass, and electronics that are incorporated into a new car. Our measure of total output includes the first two and excludes the intermediate goods to avoid double counting.

When the modern system of economic accounting was created in the 1940s, investment was defined solely as outlays by business to purchase or create machinery, vehicles, and buildings—including residential buildings.[10] All outlays by government and households were coded as consumption expenditures; nothing that government or households purchased counted as an investment. Moreover, the investment category was limited to tangible items, things that you could put your hands on.

This was a plausible way to define investment at the height of the industrial era when most people worked on farms or in factories producing tangible products such as foodstuffs, steel, and automobiles. However, now the share of the labor force that works in manufacturing and agriculture has fallen to less than 10 per cent. But instead of fundamentally rethinking their concept of investment, economists have tried to hold on to the old definition with a few added tweaks. This is similar to the epicycles that Ptolemaic astronomers introduced into their paradigm when they had trouble accurately predicting the movement of heavenly bodies. Rather than pursuing the paradigmatic leap that Galileo eventually made, they just tinkered with their incorrect framework to make it work a little bit better. Economists have done something similar with the concept of investment as they have faced an economy that is very different from that of the industrial era.

It turns out, however, that when we measure investment with an improved and theoretically coherent definition, there are some surprising results. Instead of business investment being the main driver of the economy, it is instead outlays made by government and households. This has profound implications for economic policy. For years, policy has been based on the premise that we need to limit the funds going to government and households because it is business that makes the critical investments that contribute to future prosperity. However, when measured in the U.S., business investment is less than 30 per cent of total investment, making it apparent that this policy choice has been totally misguided.

DYSFUNCTIONAL FINANCE

The existing financial infrastructure in most developed economies is rooted in the misconception that business investment is the engine that drives the economy. This infrastructure produces two extremely consequential results. First, it operates as a kind of giant vacuum cleaner that extracts resources from most people and transfers those funds to the top 1 per cent of households. Second, it systematically withholds financing for many of the productive investments that households, communities, and government should be making.

An example of the vacuum cleaner is the transformation of pension plans. In the United States and the United Kingdom, many employers have replaced defined benefit pension plans with defined contribution plans through which retirement savings are invested in corporate stocks and bonds. This adds considerable risk to retirees especially if their retirement coincides with a downturn in the stock market. Moreover, these plans generally have hidden fees that can erode the returns earned by retirees by as much as 2 or 3 per cent each year. Nevertheless, these 401(k) plans had accumulated more than $7 trillion in assets by the end of 2022.

This means that each year, these plans pour hundreds of millions of new dollars into the stock market. However, corporations collectively have been able to finance what new investments they make out of profits; these pension funds inflows are not actually needed or used to finance productive investment. However, in recent decades, a growing share of executive compensation for top corporate managers comes from stock options and stock grants. This was done in the hope that this would align the interests of top managers with shareholders.

But what has happened is that corporate leaders have dramatically increased the use of corporate funds for share buybacks, a practice that was not even legal in the U.S. before 1982. By 2022, total buybacks of shares exceeded $1 trillion. These buybacks boost the firm's share price and help assure that the compensation that executives receive in the form of stock grants and stock options will be maximized. In short, the annual inflows of retirement savings of the many facilitates the maximization of income for a small corporate elite.

At the same time, the financial system fails to direct funds into such vitally important activities as building affordable housing or supporting small businesses. The U.S. Congress created the Small Business Administration to provide loan guarantees as a way to reduce the cost of bank loans. However, even for firms that are able to jump through all the hoops, the interest rate on the loans can be forbiddingly high. Moreover, with the greater concentration in the banking industry, fewer banks involve themselves in small business lending. The problem is particularly acute for innovative small firms trying to develop new products and new processes. They are often able to get federal support for two or three years, but commercialization of a new product can take five to ten years. The time between when government support runs out and when they have a product to sell is aptly called, "the valley of death."

Instead of financing the activities that would improve habitation, the existing financial infrastructure has instead been systematically increasing income and wealth inequality. A fundamental reform of this financial infrastructure is necessary to make a habitation economy work effectively.

DEMOCRATIZING HABITATION

The final chapter lays out the kinds of reforms that are necessary for people to shape their own habitation. Reforms are needed at multiple levels: the local, subnational regions, national, supernational regions, and global. But the consistent theme of all of these reforms is to increase the capacity of people at the local level to shape the development of their own habitation. One critical element is increasing the funds that are available at the local level both by changes in how tax revenues are distributed as well as changes in the operations of the financial system.

But funds alone will not solve the problem. It is also necessary to expand democratic participation at the local level and develop new mechanisms to assure that both businesses and governments are accountable to residents. Recent experiments with participatory budgeting and citizens' assemblies suggest some of the new institutions that should be considered. But considerable experimentation will be required to figure out the most effective ways to combine elections with referenda with some of these new institutional structures.

The argument of the book, in brief, is that the understanding that we now have a habitation economy is a way to get beyond the current crisis of democratic rule. Significantly, both thinkers on the right and on the left have argued that our dual reliance on "free markets" and a strong central state has not been working either economically or politically. This has produced a deep divide between ordinary people and conventional political leaders. Without real opportunities to shape their own communities, most people are alienated from politics, have little understanding of how the political process works, and have a deep distrust of most politicians. This is the fertile ground that nourishes outsider demagogues who promise to tear down the existing political structures.

The way past this impasse is to re-engage people at the local level, and turn communities—both large and small—into training grounds in which people come to understand what they want, what they need, and the political strategies by which they can achieve their goals. This vision of a decentralized participatory democracy has deep historical roots, but it was deeply impractical in the industrial era. It was effectively marginalized by the rise of giant corporations and big governments. Today, however, with the potential for a true habitation society, this ideal has gained new power and practicality. It is, in fact, the only sure path to preserve and deepen democratic self-governance.

2

Why habitation?

Unfamiliar terms can be useful to highlight patterns that are hard to recognize with our existing vocabulary and concepts. This is the reason for using the somewhat archaic word "habitation". The dictionary definition is "the state or process of living in a particular place." The most familiar usage is to say that there are no signs of human habitation in a particular place.

I use the term to encompass all of the activities that are involved in creating, maintaining, and improving the human settlements in which we live.[1] During the Covid-19 lockdowns, we became acutely aware of the "essential workers" who made it possible for the rest of us to survive when we were confined to our own homes. Those essential workers included hospital employees, grocery and supermarket staffs, delivery people, and those keeping the phones, the internet, the electricity, and other utilities from crashing. We can think of these essential workers as the core of the habitation workforce.

But many of the others who were laid off or working from home during the lockdowns were also part of the habitation labor force. This includes construction workers building homes, offices, commercial spaces, or infrastructure projects. It also encompasses the people employed in education, childcare, and healthcare including also yoga studios, gyms, and mental health services. Moreover, those working in city government, policing, transportation, arts and entertainment, retail trade and restaurants are sustaining habitation. Finally, the growing number of people in the innovation economy who are developing new products and new processes are working to improve habitation in the future.

Most of us also do habitation work when we are not engaged in paid employment. Childrearing, cleaning house, home repairs, yard work, helping neighbors, and participation in civic groups are also part of creating, maintaining, and improving our communities. Similarly, various forms of activism to reduce environmental harms or increase the accountability of police can also be counted as doing habitation work.

The habitation concept is related to the concept of social reproduction that has been elaborated by feminist scholars. Conventional economic analyses have focused on the process of production of material goods including both agricultural and industrial products. This generates a view of the economy that is centered on men because through most of history they have done the bulk of factory and farm labor. The consequence of this approach is that much of the work done by women, often unpaid, is pushed into the background or simply ignored. Feminists, however, insist that what women have been doing—childbearing, childrearing, cooking, maintaining homes, and sustaining social ties—is equally essential to the economy. This is the work of social reproduction that is needed to sustain communities over time.

Moreover, the reality has become more complicated because for many decades, the labor of production of physical goods has been shrinking and the sphere of reproductive or habitation labor has been growing. This pattern has been going on with agriculture for centuries. In the 1820s, for example, most people both enslaved and free, worked in agriculture. By the 2020s, agriculture in the U.S. accounted for less than 1.5 per cent of the labor force. Manufacturing employment was 32 per cent of non-farm employment in 1953, but it has fallen to less than 10 per cent today.

Some of this shrinking of the manufacturing labor force is the result of businesses moving overseas to take advantage of cheaper labor in China, Vietnam, Indonesia, or Central America. But even in China—currently the world's manufacturing workshop—only about 18 per cent of employed people work in manufacturing. Ongoing technological advances across industries are replacing human beings with automated machinery in both early and late industrializing nations. In the mid-twentieth century, it was not uncommon for giant factories to employ tens of thousands of workers across multiple shifts. Today, however, factories of that size are rare and most manufacturing facilities number their employees in the hundreds.

Moreover, as the need for labor in manufacturing and agriculture has declined, there has been an enormous increase in employment in services, a heterogenous category that includes stockbrokers, hairdressers, nurses, and retail workers. The common characteristics of the service category is the production of outputs that are either intangible or temporary like a haircut or a concert. With real estate agents or retail trade, the intangibility involves shifting ownership of something from one party to another. Government data indicates that roughly 80 per cent of U.S. employees work in the service sector.

Most of these service workers can be seen as helping to produce, maintain, or improve habitation. But, of course, some are doing so in ways that have negative consequences for the quality of life of others. One can think of real estate agents who maintain patterns of racial segregation, businesses that provide payday loans at exorbitant rates, gun dealers who sell assault rifles, for-profit education and training programs that fail to deliver on their promises, and local government employees who are unresponsive to citizen needs. In short, the fact that more people are doing habitation work or service work is morally neutral; it does not automatically improve people's lives.

HABITATION AND IMPROVEMENT

The inspiration for using the habitation concept comes from the Hungarian theorist, Karl Polanyi. He was a mid-twentieth-century critic of the free-market ideas that are often labeled as neoliberalism or market fundamentalism. In his most famous book, *The Great Transformation*, Polanyi calls one of the early chapters, "Habitation versus Improvement", the only chapter where the title is in quotation marks. The source of the quotation is a pamphlet written in 1607 in England after a period of rural unrest. The unrest resulted from the practice of enclosing farm land, a practice that was common in England for several centuries.

One type of enclosure focused on land that had been set aside as an agricultural common where people, including the poor, were allowed to graze cows, sheep, and pigs. Some New England cities such as Boston have retained a common and ultimately converted it into an urban park. However, as new and more productive agricultural practices were introduced, local landowners in England sometimes took control of the common and planted it with crops. In other cases, landowners would transform fields that had been previously cultivated by their tenants into pastures for sheep. In both cases, the enclosures disrupted the habitation of the poor by cutting off part or all of their food supply. Many rural residents were forced to move elsewhere.

The author of this 1607 pamphlet proposed a compromise that would reduce the number of these enclosures. He argued that with that compromise: "The poor man shall be satisfied in his end: Habitation, and the gentlemen not hindered in his desire: Improvement."[2] Polanyi drew on this sentence to emphasize the tension between *habitation*—the residential arrangements that had sustained rural people for generations—and *improvement*, the drive to increase economic output.

Polanyi went on to argue that in the seventeenth and eighteenth centuries, the pattern of development tracked what the pamphleteer had recommended. Both the British Crown and Parliament implemented compromises that slowed the pace of enclosures, so that the rural population was able to cope with the changes. However, Polanyi's purpose was to contrast this government-imposed gradualism with what happened in the early nineteenth century when industrialization took off in England. When improvement meant the rapid increase in the number of factories that used newly developed machinery to produce textiles, the consequences for habitation were immediate and disastrous. Tens of thousands were displaced from rural areas and pushed into pestilential cities with inadequate housing, a lack of sanitation, periodic epidemics, and air filled with smoke.

With the enclosures, government had repeatedly intervened to slow down the process of improvement, giving people a chance to adjust and adapt. During the industrial revolution, however, neither the Crown nor Parliament took action to slow the pace of change. Guided by political economy's doctrine of laissez-faire, they chose to allow industrial advance—improvement—to accelerate.[3] But the rate of change was disastrous both in the countryside and in the industrial cities. It would take many decades before working people were able to reconstruct a barely adequate form of habitation.

Moreover, even when urban workers finally acquired some stability and resources through unionization and community building, they were again subject to the disruption of improvement as production moved to new factories in places where labor was cheaper and not yet organized. Once again, habitation was compromised as jobs disappeared and revenues for local government declined. Manchester, for example, had been one of the historic centers of textile production. But production peaked in 1914, and more factories were shuttered every decade thereafter. Detroit, the U.S. center of the automobile industry, followed a parallel process of deindustrialization a half century later. The city's population in 1950 was 1.8 million people. By 2021, it had fallen to 632,000.

The conflict between habitation and improvement has also played out globally as Europeans exerted their power over people on other continents. Seizing land from Indigenous populations, kidnapping people through the slave trade, and the coerced extraction of raw materials through mining and plantation agriculture disrupted and sometimes destroyed the habitation of people in Africa, Asia, the Americas, Australia and New Zealand. Polanyi emphasizes the example of Britain's imposition of head taxes on native people in their African colonies. The requirement that taxes be paid in currency forced people whose habitation was rooted in subsistence agriculture to seek paid employment that they had previously rejected. The head taxes facilitated the improvements of the colonizers who needed workers for their plantations and mines.

Polanyi's analysis of the conflict between habitation and improvement parallels the thinking of another Central European political economist, Joseph Schumpeter, who characterized capitalism as involving an ongoing process of creative destruction.[4] On the one side, improvement is creative in that it expands economic output, at least for some. At the same time, it often disrupts existing patterns of working and living. In many cases, the main thing that is destroyed is the habitation of working people.

THE CONFLICT BETWEEN HABITATION AND IMPROVEMENT TODAY

As Polanyi's example of the enclosures suggests, there have always been ways to manage and minimize the conflict between habitation and improvement. However, today when most people's work is to produce habitation and all of us consume habitation, it is possible to overcome the conflict completely. This could happen if societies invested in improvements that result in better habitation for everyone. We can see this possibility most clearly with the transition to clean energy. When improvement takes the form of increased reliance on solar, wind, and other renewable sources of power, it is possible to close down coal-burning plants that pollute the air. Fewer cases of asthma and respiratory diseases, in turn, reduces the burden on the healthcare system. Moreover, reduced carbon emissions also mean slowing climate change and reducing the frequency of extreme weather events. In short, economic improvement would also improve our habitation.

Similarly, if new technologies make it possible to construct a more efficient and more convenient urban transportation system that uses clean and renewable energy, that also would be an improvement that builds better habitation. People would waste less time commuting, making them more productive both at work and outside of work. Technological advances could also facilitate breakthroughs in construction so affordable and attractive housing could be built at significantly lower costs than at present. This would substantially upgrade the habitation of people now forced to live with long commutes or housing that absorbed half or more of their income.

Many new technologies have been provided to the public with the claim that they would make our lives better. But the reality is that the conflict between habitation and improvement has actually worsened in recent decades. While construction technologies have advanced, there is a deepening crisis of housing affordability with homeless populations increasing and many families paying too much for inadequate housing. The internet was supposed to launch a new epoch of enlightenment as vast amounts of information became immediately available, but instead we have a steep rise in disinformation, political polarization, and deteriorating mental health. Medical breakthroughs were supposed to extend longevity, and yet in recent years, life expectancy has been falling in the U.S. and the U.K.

The internet has also made possible the growth of firms such as Amazon that achieve huge economies of scale, but the consequence has been the demise of hundreds of thousands of small retail shops and the decline of many downtown shopping districts. Moreover, technological advances have led to corporations shedding both white-collar and blue-collar workers, leaving many once vibrant communities in severe decline. Perhaps, most critically, while we now have a fleet of technologies that could facilitate a rapid phasing out of all fossil fuels, we continue to spend billions each year to mine coal and pump petroleum out of the earth even as the costs of climate change mount in droughts, unpredictable and severe weather events, extreme temperatures, and rising sea levels.

Why has the possibility of overcoming the conflict between habitation and improvement not been realized? Why is it that the conflict is intensifying rather than easing? That is the big question that this book seeks to answer. Much of the problem is that we are continuing to understand, manage, and govern a habitation economy with the intellectual tools that were developed in the industrial era. More specifically, we are using industrial-era economics to organize an economy that has ceased being industrial. Intensifying conflict between habitation and improvement is the direct consequence of that mistaken approach.

OTHER VIRTUES OF THE HABITATION CONCEPT

We shall come back to the issue of why the conflict between habitation and improvement is worsening, but there are several other points to be made about the value of the habitation concept. Viewing the economy through the lens of habitation helps us to see some of the problems with most economic analysis. This point follows logically from another important idea developed by Polanyi. He insisted that there are two distinct ways to think about the economy: the formal and the substantive.[5] The formal is the approach of mainstream economists who focus on the rules and procedures that facilitate the optimal use of scarce resources. The substantive approach, in contrast, examines the full range of measures through which societies secure the goods and services needed to survive and flourish.

The formal approach concentrates on the buying and selling of commodities and the workings of various markets that connect economic actors. The substantivist approach is broader because it looks at all of the different ways that things of economic value are produced. One of Polanyi's key points is that before the rise of market society in the nineteenth century, one could not make sense of how people fulfilled their material needs by deploying the conceptual apparatus of formal economics. While some individuals might have been maximizing their utility, their calculations were not the factor that determined how the economy worked. The substantive economy was embedded in and shaped by inherited cultural beliefs and political power. For example, preindustrial societies sometimes had marketplaces to distribute goods, but prices were usually fixed by custom or edict rather than fluctuating with supply and demand.

Polanyi recognizes that the formal approach to economics had value for understanding the market economy that emerged in the nineteenth century. Much of the dramatic expansion of output from farms and factories could be explained within a framework that focused on maximizing returns from the use of scarce resources. And yet, Polanyi also emphasizes that the formal approach to market economies was insufficient because it did not understand the ways in which the market economy remained dependent on the household, the natural environment, the state, and specific patterns of interpersonal behavior.[6]

The concept of habitation helps us to recognize the substantive nature of our contemporary economy because it highlights how important to our current quality of life are things that are not bought and sold like standardized commodities. For example, some of the major expenditures in family budgets are for things that are very different from standard commodities. These include housing, both for renters and owners, the cost of childcare, the cost of elder care, and the cost of higher education. And for the U.S., the list also includes the considerable cost of healthcare: health insurance, prescription drugs, and uncovered outlays. Moreover, all of these expenditures are central to people's quality of life.

Moreover, the housing that people can afford is not just an issue of whether they face homelessness or have to make do with limited indoor and outdoor space. There is the question of the stability of their housing solution. Will shifts in family income or increases in rent or mortgage payments, or unanticipated repairs necessitate another move? There are also questions of the desirability or undesirability of the particular neighborhood where the housing is located. How safe is it in terms of crime or environmental hazards? What kind of services and amenities are nearby or require time-consuming travel? How close or far is it to relevant workplaces? As housing prices have risen, many people are left with punishingly long commutes both to and from work.

The importance of access to good quality healthcare hardly needs elaboration. There are millions of people in the U.S. who cannot afford their prescribed medications or needed medical procedures. The same can be said for access to decent quality childcare. Family members, usually mothers, will often have to limit their hours of work and infants and small children might end up being parked in front of the television without the kind of stimulation that is optimal for their cognitive and emotional development. Similarly, the absence of affordable options for taking care of elderly family members suffering from dementia or disabilities puts enormous strain on family budgets of both money and time.

Finally, access to higher education can be critical for achieving upward mobility. However, $1.77 trillion of accumulated student loan debt in the U.S. as of 2023 places a heavy burden on many individuals. Moreover, the necessity of debt financing means that many young people from households in the bottom half of the income distribution do not choose to pursue higher education. After all, there is no certainty that earning a degree will yield a well-paying job. It is possible that even if they successfully complete a degree, their post-college income, adjusted for debt repayment, might not exceed what they could make without a college education. And if they are unable to complete college, their accumulated debt could make them worse off than if they had skipped college.

Moreover, some of the most important aspects of well-being are not reflected in income statistics. There is the critical question of economic security: how great is the risk that a household might face a 50 per cent or greater reduction in income from one year to the next due to illness, accident, unemployment, family breakup or other circumstance.[7] There is the question of the non-pecuniary benefits or defects of the job one has: employment security, whether the work is sometimes enjoyable or intellectually engaging, and whether it provides for positive and rewarding interactions with others. And then there are issues of personal safety, risks of discrimination or mistreatment by others, and the quality of the air one breathes and the water one drinks.

In sum, the conventional or formal economic framework concentrates our attention on one variable: the amount of income earned by households. However, the habitation concept reminds us that the amount of income is only one of many variables that determine one's quality of life. And many of these other variables are not issues of individual choice, but rather they are issues of collective consumption and public policies.

HABITATION AS SYNTHESIS

The habitation concept also draws on and helps to integrate four of the most important critiques of economic modernity: the feminist critique, the environmental critique, the indigenous critique, and the moral critique. The *feminist argument* has focused on the neglect by economists of the market economy's dependence on what goes on in the household: childbearing, childrearing, house work, and care work. And yet, most of economics has largely ignored this work; unpaid labor performed by family members is still not included in GDP. The British economist, Arthur Pigou, long ago quipped that if a man married his housekeeper, it would reduce national income since her labor would no longer be compensated with a wage.

The habitation concept seeks to make reproductive labor more central to our understanding of the economy, whether it is paid or unpaid. As the labor force participation of married women has increased, there has been a parallel expansion in the number of care work jobs in the economy. And yet, much of this care work including childcare and elder care is both expensive because it is labor intensive and poorly compensated because it is work that is often done by women of color and immigrants. The consequence is an ongoing care crisis as many cannot afford the care they need and care workers continue to be exploited.

The *environmental argument* emphasizes the mistaken industrial-era belief that the byproducts of production could simply be dumped on the land, in the air, or into waterways. Human dependence on unpolluted air, water, and land was simply ignored in the race for improvement or increased economic output. The habitation concept, in contrast, recognizes that we live in particular places that are the habitat for both ourselves and many species of plants, animals, and other life forms. In an era of climate change and frequent climate-driven disasters, it is abundantly clear that our survival requires reversing the damage that current and past generations have done to the natural environment.

The *indigenous argument* parallels and long predates the environmental one. Native Americans and other Indigenous peoples have emphasized the necessity of living in harmony with the natural environment. They have understood their dependence on nature and their obligation to be stewards of the places they inhabit. The Spanish term *"vivir bien"*—living well—is a rough translation of words used by native people of the Andes region in South America to express this idea of a life in harmony with nature. This idea has become an important part of political mobilization by Indigenous groups against political elites focused on maximizing economic output regardless of the consequences.

Finally, the *moral critique* insists that economic doctrines that glorify the individual's effort to pursue their own interest, as in the maximizing of profit, threatens to erode the moral sentiments that hold communities together. What happens to norms of reciprocity or the golden rule when each person is out for him or herself? This argument can be traced back to Adam Smith's *Theory of Moral Sentiments* where he argues that even a foot race requires rules that prevent runners from deliberately fouling their competitors. It follows that the pursuit of self-interest by the butcher, the brewer or the baker, as famously mentioned in *The Wealth of Nations*, must occur within a system of rules and enforcement that penalizes those who commit fouls.[8]

The habitation concept helps us recognize that our current extremely complex division of labor maximizes our dependence on others. We saw this most dramatically during the height of the Covid pandemic when people applauded the essential workers laboring in hospitals, grocery stores, and delivery vehicles. Sustaining this mutual dependence becomes ever more difficult with the deepening inequalities of income and wealth that characterize the current era. In fact, we see the extremely rich trying to escape from this mutual dependence by sheltering themselves on private islands or yachts the size of small battleships. When we think of the economy instead in terms of habitation, it leads us to value communities that are inclusive and built around mutual recognition and norms of reciprocity.

WHAT PEOPLE WANT

A premise of my argument is that most people in developed market societies are not getting the habitation that they want or need. On what basis am I making that claim? Since habitation is an unfamiliar term and it is multi-dimensional, there is no simple way to assess how satisfied people are with their current habitation. Nevertheless, if one looks at public attitudes on key elements of habitation, it is clear that large majorities would prefer something different from what they have now.

In terms of housing, a 2022 survey in the U.S. by the libertarian Cato Institute found that 34 per cent of respondents were extremely concerned, 27 per cent were very concerned, and another 26 per cent were somewhat concerned with the cost of housing.[9] Some 73 per cent of respondents indicated that an average person could not afford to buy a house in the respondent's area. And 69 per cent of respondents who had children expressed worry that their children or grandchildren would be unable to afford a home. Moreover 63 per cent of all respondents said they would favor building more housing if it would make it easier for low-income people to live in their neighborhood.

Problems with the care economy are also pervasive. In a Harris survey of 2,519 adults in early 2023, 60 per cent of respondents gave the U.S. healthcare system a grade of C or lower, 61 per cent reported affordability is a barrier to getting the care they need, and 66 per cent complained that healthcare providers appeared more rushed than they had in the past.[10] A Kaiser Family Foundation survey of 1,573 U.S. adults in 2022 found that of those who had either stayed in a long-term care facility or had helped a loved one seeking such care, 62 per cent said it was either somewhat difficult or very difficult to find an appropriate facility and the same number reported the difficulty of affording such care.[11] A Morning Consult poll of 2,200 adults in June, 2023 reported that 56 per cent of parents reported the difficulty of finding affordable, high-quality childcare or after-school care, and 78 per cent of parents said they would be more likely to support a political candidate who promised to increase affordable childcare options.[12]

Similar majorities also express reservations about other dimensions of habitation. A Pew Research Center poll of 5,115 respondents in June of 2023 reports that between 59–61 per cent of respondents consider gun violence, crime, and drug addiction to be big problems in the U.S.[13] The American Community Life Survey from the American Enterprise Institute interviewed 5,058 respondents in 2021 and found that only 36 per cent lived in neighborhoods that were high or very high in amenities such as stores, restaurants, parks, or other recreation areas. Surprisingly, whether residents lived in big cities, small cities, suburbs of big cities, suburbs of small cities, or towns, a majority of respondents would prefer to live elsewhere. The exception were rural residents, 72 per cent of whom expressed a preference to live in a rural area. In this survey, only 9 per cent of respondents felt that they had much say in decisions made about their neighborhood.[14]

Another Pew study of environmental attitudes that surveyed 10,329 adults in the U.S. in mid-2023 found significant partisan divisions on issues of climate change. Nevertheless, two-thirds of respondents placed a higher priority on developing alternative energy sources as opposed to expanding production of fossil fuels. The same study found that 63 per cent of respondents felt that the government was not doing enough to protect the water quality of lakes, rivers, and streams, and 58 per cent felt that government efforts for clean air were insufficient. Seventy-five per cent said that the federal government had some role to play in addressing the variation in environmental health risks across different communities.[15]

Finally, a survey of 2001 respondents in early 2023 by Smart Growth America found 63 per cent of respondents reporting that traffic was a problem where they lived; 53 per cent reported that on most days, they need to travel to other neighborhoods for work, school, or shopping. They also found that 71 per cent of respondents either somewhat agreed or strongly agreed that the government's priority on building highways had shortchanged options such as trains, buses, cycle lanes, and sidewalks.[16]

In sum, whether we are talking about housing, local amenities, care, the environment or infrastructure, many people's habitation is falling short of what they would like to have.

THE WORSENING CONFLICT BETWEEN HABITATION AND IMPROVEMENT

My argument is that people are not getting the habitation that they want because our societies are continuing to manage a habitation economy with the tools and institutional structures of the industrial era. But I am not arguing that this ongoing mistake is a product simply of intellectual inertia or laziness. Rather, it has been the result of real political conflicts in which existing economic interests have fought ferociously to prevent a shift in the conceptual frameworks used to understand society and economy. The crucial decade of that fight was the 1970s. Back then, a number of leading intellectuals in the U.S. and Europe argued that our societies were undergoing a shift away from industrialism towards something different. Some called this a postindustrial society, some called it a knowledge economy, some called it an information economy.[17] However, most analysts focused on the central role of scientific advances in the economy, the shift of higher education from a small elite to a large percentage of young people, the growing role of services in the economy, and the development of computer technology.

It was common among these thinkers to argue that some of the social movements and political turmoil of the 1960s and early 1970s could be understood as a symptom of this postindustrial transition. They also shared the fundamental insight that the shifts in social organization that they were analyzing required a rethinking of inherited economic ideas. Many of them suggested that government would inevitably have to play more of a role in the economy.

Unfortunately, these postindustrial thinkers are barely remembered today because a different group of intellectuals triumphed in the political battles of that period. The winners were the free-market theorists led by Friedrich Hayek and Milton Friedman. Their central argument was that the growing economic difficulties of Western economies in the 1970s were the consequence of decades of too much governmental interference into markets. Their solutions, embraced by Ronald Reagan and Margaret Thatcher, were to cut taxes, cut public spending, and cut government regulation of business.[18]

There was little direct confrontation or argument between postindustrial thinkers and free-market theorists even though their diagnoses and analyses were radically at odds. The postindustrial theorists argued that the economy had changed fundamentally and that more government was necessary. The free-market thinkers insisted that it simply did not matter if the mix of economic outputs had changed, the problem was that an unnecessary expansion of government had unfortunately reduced society's reliance on the power of the market to coordinate economic decisions.[19] In fact, the free-market theorists simply ignored the postindustrial analysts because of the mismatch in their institutional support. The postindustrial thinkers were individual scholars without institutional backing. Some of the existing liberal think tanks might occasionally invite one of them to present their ideas, but there was no postindustrial think tank dedicated to spreading these ideas.

On the other side, however, there was a network of free-market think tanks that worked night and day to get free-market ideas into wide circulation.[20] Even more importantly, large sections of the business community in the U.K. and the U.S. decided in the 1970s that embracing the Hayek–Friedman theoretical agenda was the best way to head off the threat of increased government regulation of business.[21] When politicians such as Reagan and Thatcher embraced the free-market agenda, they were assured devoted support from the business community.

That victory in the war of ideas proved extraordinarily durable. The hegemony of free-market ideas survived even the global financial crisis of 2008–09 that was a direct result of its mistaken ideas about financial regulation. While some thinkers continued to develop and elaborate postindustrial thinking across this period, postindustrial ideas had little influence on politics or political debates.

Ironically, there was a brief period in the 1990s when the emergence of the internet led many people to embrace the idea that a fundamentally new economy had emerged and required a rethinking of public policies. The boom in internet stocks in the last half of the decade was driven by enthusiasm for the transformative potential of the new technologies. However, in contrast to postindustrial theory, that version of a "new economy" was tied to a libertarian politics that claimed technology had made government essentially irrelevant and unnecessary.

THE POSTINDUSTRIAL TRUTHS

It is important a half-century later to understand how much the postindustrial theorists got right and how they correctly anticipated some of the key changes that have transformed developed market societies. They recognized that the shrinking of the agricultural labor force over two hundred years would be replicated in a shorter time period with manufacturing. These theorists anticipated that while manufacturing work had been the largest share of employment in developed nations in the 1940s and 1950s, it would also experience a rapid decline as ever more sophisticated automation reduced the need for human labor.

They correctly anticipated the processes of deindustrialization that would radically shrink the automobile workforce in Detroit and in similar industrial cities around the world. However, these analysts did not expect manufacturing to disappear. The argument was instead that in the industrial era, farming began looking more like manufacturing; it became larger scale with more mechanization and more standardization. In the postindustrial era, manufacturing would increasingly resemble many service industries. It would become more dependent on highly skilled employees and its output would be more flexible and less standardized.

Daniel Bell was the most systematic of these postindustrial theorists and he correctly anticipated three other specific developments. First, the economy would become more dependent upon advances in science and technology with computers and computerization being a particularly important driver of that process. Second, there would need to be an expanded role of government in driving technological change since businesses could not be expected to carry the high costs of fundamental research. Third, the economy's need for educated labor would continue to expand. It was not just that one needed a lot of scientists and engineers with advanced degrees, but that the average worker would need higher levels of literacy and numeracy to do their jobs effectively. The expectation was that the number of jobs relying on brute strength and an elementary school education would continue to fall. Each of these predictions has been vindicated. Let's consider each one in more detail.

Growing technological complexity

It is not just that the economy has become more dependent on science and technology. Computerization and other technological advances have produced a dramatic turn away from the standardization of products that was a central feature of the industrial age. This has been a complex process that has been driven by multiple factors. Some significant subset of consumers simply lost their taste for standardized products. One can see this clearly in the evolution of the market for such basic products as bread, beer, and coffee. In the 1950s and 1960s, markets were often dominated by a handful of big producers each of which focused on one or two heavily advertised products. In the ensuing decades, consumer demand shifted and has sought much greater variety.

Think of coffee. As recently as the 1960s, people in the U.S. and the U.K. would buy cans of ground coffee from Maxwell House or Lyon's and use a percolator to prepare a pot of coffee. Today, they are far more likely to grind gourmet beans at home or go to one of many coffee shops to order an espresso, latte, or cappuccino. In the case of beer, the market is still dominated by a handful of big brewers, but their efforts are spread out across many different labels, some of which are disguised as the work of startup firms making beer in small batches.

A similar pattern operates with all types of products. As of January 2023, Amazon was selling 12 million distinct products. Whether one is looking for a stove hood, a pool table, or an electric screwdriver, one runs into an enormous variety of choices at different price points and with different capabilities. And, of course, in the ever-growing market for entertainment products, whether we are talking books, movies, television shows, music, and games, the demand for things that are new and different is a constant theme, even while the market for certain "classical" items remains robust.

Another reason for the shift is that businesses are competing with a well-stocked and efficient market for second-hand goods. Unless a brand-new item has some obvious superiority over a used model, many consumers will be tempted to look for the item at a second-hand store or listed on an internet site. In other words, producers who do not change their products are competing for sales with their own products from earlier years.

But the most critical factor is that computerized production technologies have significantly reduced the cost disadvantage of creating differentiated products. It used to be that the cost differentiation between producing 100,000 of one item versus 10,000 of ten different variations would be very large, requiring that differentiated items sold at a much higher price than standardized ones. But now computerization makes it possible for firms to organize production lines more flexibly, and this means that differentiated products require a smaller price differential to maintain profitability.

The consequence is that many firms are in the innovation business; they are looking constantly for ways to modify their product lines and to find process improvements that would allow them to lower costs and increase profits. This is true even of a high proportion of firms that enjoy insulation from competition because they control platforms or they are able to use intellectual property rights to monopolize particular markets. For example, both the biggest tech firms and Big Pharma firms are continually searching for innovations. With tech firms, there is constant fear that upstart competitors could erode their advantage. With Big Pharma, there is the fear that patent protection on bestselling drugs will run out before they develop other new blockbuster drugs.

This search for innovation also extends into the service-producing sectors of the economy. Financial firms are looking for new financial instruments that might be attractive to investors, many hospitals are looking to capitalize on new imaging techniques or new medical procedures, and firms providing communications services need to keep up with competitors.

Increased role for government

In the mid-twentieth century, the route to innovation was to set up one's own laboratory and hire scientists and engineers to devise new products and new processes. Bell Labs, in particular, was extraordinarily successful in producing innovations that were critical to the development of electronics and communications. But other corporate laboratories could also boast of strings of innovations and improvements in existing products. However, in the twenty-first century, the stand-alone corporate laboratory has ceased to be the main location for corporate innovation.

The main explanation is the growing technological complexity of contemporary innovation. In industry after industry, breakthroughs increasingly require bringing together expertise from multiple different scientific and engineering specialties. At the extreme end, think of the variety of experts who must be mobilized to develop the next generation of smart phones for Apple and Samsung. But even far humbler products increasingly require the assembly of teams of experts. For example, the National Football League has been working with industry to develop helmets that will do a better job of protecting players from the repeated head injuries that lead to chronic traumatic encephalopathy. This involves neuroscientists, materials expertise, physicists who analyze impacts, and mastery of a range of computer-based technologies.[22]

It is simply impractical for firms to assemble these teams in their in-house laboratories. For one thing, it is too expensive to create separate career tracks for technologists from five to ten different disciplines. For another, the more creative technologists are not drawn to spending many years working in the same corporation where they might have little control over the projects to which they are assigned. And firms are less likely to innovate with the less creative technologists who might be attracted to a career at the same firm.

Moreover, these issues of complexity typically persist throughout the life cycle of product development. More complicated products are usually more difficult to produce at a reasonable price, so it is likely that a mix of different technical specialties will be needed even after the firm has completed an innovative product and is moving towards mass production. A considerable body of work has shown that the global pattern of innovative firms has been to co-locate research and development and actual production because of the need for ongoing intellectual exchanges between people assigned to these different functions.

Firms handle this complexity by reversing the movement towards vertical integration that had created the giant corporations of the twentieth century. In industry after industry, we have seen a movement away from vertical integration towards collaborative network production. Collaborative network production takes a variety of different forms, but the core characteristic is that very large corporations depend on networks of smaller producers with very specific types of expertise. In the automotive industry, Toyota pioneered setting up an auto assembly plant surrounded by production facilities for subcontracting firms who provided just-in-time delivery of most of the key components of the vehicle. In Hollywood, movie production has been organized as collaborations among different small firms that develop the script, contract with the talent, arrange the editing, organize the sound, and then one of the large studios does the marketing and the management of delivering the film to consumers through movie theaters or television. In the pharmaceutical industry, many of the new drugs are developed by smaller, specialized firms, who then contract with the larger established firms to finance the clinical trials and organize the marketing to physicians and consumers. In the computer industry, much of the cutting-edge software is open source with non-profit foundations coordinating the initiatives of multiple programmers, some of whom work for large firms, some for small firms, and some as individual entrepreneurs. With a variety of manufactured products, one company designs a product and then contracts with another that has expertise in manufacturing. This is the model that Apple has used with production of the iPhone being done by Foxconn in China.

Collaborative network production involves significant risks and costs. It can be difficult to find good network partners when expertise is spread out across the globe. Moreover, the potential partners one finds might either not have the competencies that they claim to have or they might not be trustworthy or both. Since innovative products generally involve intellectual property, the danger is real that one's network partners might steal the most important ideas and claim them as their own. Writing good contracts is not adequate protection because litigation takes up valuable time when firms are racing to get products to the market. There is also the scenario in which the more powerful firm shifts from cooperation to exploiting their network partners by paying far less for the services.

The consequence is that collaborative network arrangements fail when firms are unable to find trustworthy and competent partners.[23] It turns out, however, that one way to reduce the incidence of network failures is to put referees out on the field. The referees need to be disinterested parties who have the goal of facilitating effective network connections. These referees can perform three distinct services that help reduce network failures. First, they can use their own knowledge base and networks to help facilitate connections between appropriate partners. Second, they can vouch for the competence of potential partners and they can help develop training programs to increase the supply of people with the appropriate competencies.

Third, they serve as honest brokers between different partners and potentially discourage malfeasance or predatory behavior. Sometimes these referees work for non-profit agencies as with the non-profit foundations that oversee some of the major opensource software projects. However, the most effective referees tend to be the ones who have the backing of government agencies since they are more likely to have the resources to fund training programs and to have greater clout to discourage predatory behavior within network partnerships.

So, for example, in 1992 when the U.S. Department of Energy partnered with several corporations to work on a new generation of gas turbines that would increase efficiency by burning natural gas at much higher temperatures, they also included a collaboration with Clemson University to establish a research and training program that also involved researchers at other universities.[24] The goal was to promote both research and training that would facilitate more effective network collaborations.

Similarly, the program officers with the government's Small Business Innovation Research program also work to establish effective partnerships between small business firms and others, including the largest defense contractors. Several of the SBIR programs in the military sponsor speed-dating sessions between defense contractors and SBIR award winners where the smaller firms have the opportunity to pitch their innovations. If an SBIR firm alleges that a defense contractor copied their idea without compensation, the Department of Defense uses the small firm's SBIR application as proof of concept and it will impose sanctions on the contractor if it finds inappropriate behavior.[25]

It has long been the reality that the government's role in technological innovation is much greater than most analysts have been willing to acknowledge. The computer revolution would not have happened without the initial governmental investments during the Second World War in creating computational machines, its substantial purchases of early mainframe computers, and the Defense Advanced Research Projects Agency's (DARPA) critical role in the 1960s in funding the creation of computer science departments and in supporting the efforts at Xerox Parc Laboratory that made the personal computer possible.[26]

Even going back to the nineteenth century, the government has also either directly funded or subsidized the investments in infrastructure that have made possible major advances in transportation and communications technologies. And since the Second World War, the government has provided much of the funding for educating and supporting the very substantial numbers of PhD scientists and engineers working in the U.S. Without this enormous talent pool, there would not be a comparable flow of innovations.

Nevertheless, recent decades have cemented two major structural changes. The first is that innovation has become central to almost every industry in the economy; businesses that are unwilling to change what they produce and how they produce it are increasingly doomed to irrelevance. The second is that an increasingly large share of the important innovations are developed and nurtured in government-funded laboratories or research centers. In many of these settings, technologists working for private firms work side by side with publicly-funded researchers. Moreover, employees at these laboratories play an increasingly important role in helping firms make the effective network connections that will help them bring new products into the marketplace.

Expanded role of educated labor

This final part of Daniel Bell's prediction is not controversial since it is widely appreciated that across all of the developed market societies, there has been a dramatic increase in the share of the population that receives at least a college education. Germany, for example, has been unusually successful in maintaining a large share of employment in manufacturing. In 2022, manufacturing was still 23.6 per cent of all employment. Nevertheless, German manufacturers are increasingly hiring college graduates rather than people who have learned skills in apprenticeship programs. The U.S. has now fallen behind many other developed nations: as of 2022, 51.3 per cent of people in the U.S. aged between 25–34 had completed tertiary education. For South Korea, Japan, and Canada, the comparable figure is higher than 65 per cent.[27]

While higher education has expanded in most countries, there is, however, little consensus about its proper content or how it should be paid for. In the U.S., what students learn about race and gender has become a major focus of the culture wars. In the U.K., there are incentives for students to pursue degree tracks that are either scientific or vocational. Moreover, the U.K. is notorious for its Research Excellence Framework that is intended to maximize the scholarly output of its professors. However, it has frequently been criticized as providing incentives for scholars to publish the same findings in multiple articles to maximize their opportunities for advancement.

While differences across countries in the financing of higher education are substantial, funding has often become a contested issue. In the U.S., the reliance on tuition payments has pushed student loan debt to more than $1.7 trillion. Moreover, increased costs to attend public universities have severely limited access for young people coming from poorer households. In the U.K., limited government funding and a declining inflow of international students has placed severe budgetary pressures on all but the small number of well-financed and globally prominent institutions.

HOW WRONG CONCEPTS UNDERMINE HABITATION

The continuing appeal of free-market ideas helps explain why we have not come up with new policy frameworks to manage a habitation economy. However, social and economic policies derived from mistaken or archaic concepts actually intensify the conflict between habitation and improvement. Here is one example. We have come to think of housing as just another commodity where the price mechanism will balance supply and demand. In fact, we have gone further, we have conceptualized housing both as shelter and as another type of financial asset.[28]

But housing is definitely not a commodity like pork bellies or bushels of wheat. Real estate developers, whether they are building single family homes or apartment buildings face considerable uncertainty given the extended time period between initial planning and the completion of construction. Both weather events and economic downturns add further levels of risk. The obvious way to handle this uncertainty is to build for the high end of the real estate market where larger profit margins can offset both anticipated and unanticipated costs. In theory, as more affluent people move into these homes, their earlier housing will trickle down to others. But housing in expensive neighborhoods will remain expensive, many of the rich accumulate multiple residences, and still others are turned into short-term rental options for tourists. The result is an ever-greater shortage of affordable housing.

At the same time, thinking of housing as a new asset class fueled dramatic growth in mortgage borrowing in many countries. This turned disastrous when the long rise in housing prices suddenly stopped. In fact, the spectacular growth in subprime mortgage lending in the United States was the immediate cause of the 2008–09 global financial crisis. Moreover, the crisis produced a huge wave of foreclosures in the

U.S. This was a powerful demonstration that thinking of housing as an asset class rather than a way to provide shelter for the population is a good way to create ever-more precarious habitation.

This is just one example of the very real consequences of mistaken ideas. Despite the fact that we now have a real opportunity to overcome the historic conflict between habitation and improvement, we are instead experiencing an ongoing degradation of our habitation that, in turn, fuels more political discontent and polarization. It is imperative that we begin to ask better questions to open up new political and economic possibilities. But to do this, we have to clear away the thickets of obsolete ideas that have been carried over uncritically from the past. This is the task of the next four chapters.

3

Commodification without commodities

Our habitation economy remains largely invisible because of the consensus that our society is organized around a market economy. The problem is that a market economy is defined as one in which people buy and sell commodities. However, most of the things that we consume today are not similar to the items that economists have labeled as commodities. The factory that Adam Smith described in *The Wealth of Nations* made pins and David Ricardo's analysis of international trade focused on cloth and wine. Their analyses depended on a definition of commodities as standardized goods that are available from many different producers. Moreover, they also assume a transaction between buyer and seller that was a one-shot transaction rather than a long-term relationship.

Karl Polanyi noted 80 years ago that three of the core elements of an economy—land, labor, and money—are fictitious commodities because they were not produced to be sold on a market. Land is nature subdivided into parcels of different sizes, labor is the activity of human beings, and the supply of money is generally carefully regulated by central banks. It follows that the supply and demand for these key economic inputs cannot possibly be equilibrated by ongoing changes in prices. In a word, Polanyi shows that the existence of these fictitious commodities undermines the claim that a market economy could be a self-regulating structure.

The argument here builds on Polanyi, but it is somewhat different. Polanyi was effectively distinguishing between the process of commodification and the production of actual commodities. Society creates a market for labor where the work of human beings is effectively commodified, but this project of commodification does not actually transform labor into a commodity that is equivalent to a bushel of wheat or a ton of steel. Labor remains a fictitious commodity even as we pretend that the labor market is just like any other commodity market.

The point is that almost anything can be commodified. We have seen that happen with trips into outer space, nonfungible tokens, and the service of surrogates to carry a fertilized egg to childbirth. In fact, most forms of care—childcare, healthcare, eldercare—can be purchased on the market. However, the fact that something is commodified does not magically transform it into a standardized good transferred between buyer and seller in a single moment. This is important because in a habitation economy most of the things that we consume—housing, healthcare, education, transportation, energy, and other services—do not fit this definition because the products are not standardized or are not available from many different producers or are not transferred in a single moment in time.[1]

A specific example should suffice to make the point. Pharmaceutical companies in the U.S. insist that government must not interfere with the prices they establish for their products. They invoke economics to say that the interplay of supply and demand will assure that prices are set at the appropriate level. But that claim was made for true commodities: standardized products available from multiple producers. A patent-protected drug that is the only effective treatment for a particular condition is not standardized and it is available from only one firm to whom the government has granted a monopoly through the patent system.

In short, the arguments that celebrate the price mechanism as an instrument that balances supply and demand depend on things being true commodities. If, for example, there is a spike in the price of eggs for some reason, two things are likely to happen. First, some of the people who usually buy eggs will shift to other products; they will eat yogurt or cereal for breakfast instead. Second, seeing the high price that eggs are commanding, farmers will acquire more egg-laying hens. The consequence of demand easing and supply increasing means that the price of eggs is likely to return to something closer to its historic level within months. Those who celebrate the market also emphasize the ease with which consumers can discipline producers. If, for example, one producer's eggs are not properly washed before packaging, creating a risk of food poisoning, they are likely to see a precipitous drop in demand.

The price mechanism assumes multiple producers of a standardized product, so consumers can switch and so that expanding the supply is likely to occur. It also has to be relatively easy for purchasers to either substitute another product or simply do without. So, for example, when gasoline prices rise, those with long automobile commutes cannot really curtail their demand. Finally, it really helps the adjustment process if the transfer of the product occurs both instantly and repeatedly as happens with most grocery products.

It is not surprising that economists have put commodities at the center of their understanding of modern economies. After all, economic development over the last five hundred years saw the creation of global markets for standardized products including gold, silver, spices, sugar, rum, cotton, wool, wine, tobacco, lumber, wheat, and then textiles, apparel, shoes, soap, iron, steel, and so on. When modern economics was created in the nineteenth century, the production of these classical commodities represented a very substantial share of economic output.

However, in our current habitation economy, while we still make use of many of these products, they represent a much-diminished share of the basket of goods and services that most people consume. While most of the things we consume have been effectively commodified, they differ from classical commodities either because they are not standardized and there are not multiple producers, or substitution is difficult, or the transactions are not immediate and frequent.

U.S. data reports on how personal consumption expenditures were divided among different types of outlays (see Table 3.1) These are total outlays that aggregate together all households. However, consumption patterns are very different for the top 1 per cent of households. They tend to have large staffs for their multiple homes to clean, to cook, to manage the grounds, to keep the books, and pilot and maintain the yachts. These employees are included in the data in the relevant service category. The bottom 20 per cent of households, in contrast, usually spend a very large share of their income on housing and food.

Table 3.1 Personal consumption expenditures by major type of product

Personal consumption expenditure	Billions ($)	Percentage
Goods	6,191.50	33.3
Durable goods	2,198.80	11.8
Nondurable goods	3,992.70	21.5
Services	12,379.20	66.7
Housing and utilities	3,278.70	17.7
Healthcare	2,999.60	16.2
Transportation	604.20	3.3
Recreation	716.30	3.9
Food services and accommodation	1,367.40	7.4
Financial services and insurance	1,321.90	7.1
Other	1,540.60	8.3
Final consumption expenditures of nonprofit institutions serving households (NPISHs)[a]	550.40	3.0
	18,570.60	

Source: BEA, *National Income and Product Accounts*, Table 2.3.5.

[a] Net expenses of NPISHs, defined as their gross operating expenses less primary sales to households.

Nevertheless, the overall pattern is very clear. Service outlays are generally more than double the outlays for goods. Moreover, the costs of housing, utilities, and healthcare—the core of the habitation economy—represent more than half of all service expenditures. Outlays for higher education and private schools are included in the "other services category" along with lawyers, architects, interior designers, barbers, and hair stylists.[2] Food services and accommodations—restaurants, hotels, and other temporary housing—along with recreation services that includes country clubs, tourist attractions, and entertainment, have been growing as a share of consumption over recent decades.

The point, however, is that the share of classical commodities in current consumption is very small. Almost all of the service outlays are not standardized but customized for each individual, and most of them involve transactions that extend over time. Moreover, even with goods, there has been a dramatic shift away from standardization with consumers being offered products with varying characteristics at many different price levels. Furthermore, many purchases of goods now extend over time with warranties and ongoing service contracts. All of these shifts away from classical commodities end up disempowering consumers relative to providers.

THE DECLINE OF STANDARDIZATION

Henry Ford pioneered several key features of the industrial era. He was a key practitioner of realizing the economies of scale that came from standardizing products. He is alleged to have said of the Model T that people can get it in "Any color the customer wants, as long as it's black." However, his moment of offering such limited choices did not last very long. General Motors quickly challenged Ford's domination of the automotive industry by creating a differentiated product line with vehicles at significantly different price points. It did not take long for further differentiation, so that whether you were buying a Chevrolet or a Cadillac, you could buy it with multiple options that usually added to the cost. From there, the process of product differentiation accelerated with businesses constantly adding new features to their offering to make them different from those of competitors.[3]

By the start of the twenty-first century, it was Business 101 doctrine that it was folly to be producing something that resembled a standardized commodity. The risk was high that producers overseas using cheaper labor could sell it at a lower price. The way to avoid this was by offering consumers a greater variety of choices, essentially destandarizing the product. We can call this the Baskin-Robbins strategy after the ice cream company that offers customers a choice among 31 different flavors, some of which are experimental additions that the company might add to the lineup if demand remains strong. We see a similar process in various supermarket aisles where the dominant firms constantly expand their offerings with new options.

Destandardization accelerated with advances in automation technology that significantly reduced the cost of using the same production lines to produce a variety of different products. In the beer industry, for example, the development of technology for micro-breweries made it possible to lower the cost of beers that were made in relatively small quantities. But even with the growth of micro-breweries, the global beer industry continues to be dominated by a few giant firms, one of which boasts 300 distinct brands and another offers 100 distinct brands, with many of these brands offering a range of different choices.

These technological advances have facilitated "mass customization" in a variety of industries. Some computer companies and some automobile firms allow customers to choose the specific mix of features that they want, and their particular computer or car will come off the production line made to order. A growing number of firms in the apparel industry are using similar technology to produce bespoke outfits at substantially lower price points than hand-crafted clothing. We can expect similar developments to spread to other industries since using the internet to link consumers directly to the factory eliminates many of the costs associated with wholesalers and retailers.

Destandardization is also characteristic of the service sector. One service that has always loomed large in individual budgets—housing—whether rented or owned, is perennially destandardized by size, style, and location. With relatively few exceptions, most other services are supposed to be customized to meet the needs of each particular consumer. Even in very large public universities, each student gets to choose a particular set of classes and has at least the theoretical possibility of forming connections with specific instructors who could nurture the student's individual talents. Similarly, legal or financial services or mental health services are intended to respond to the specific circumstances and needs of the individual client. Financial institutions market themselves with claims to be uniquely attentive to the interests of each client.

These non-standardized services have nevertheless been completely commodified. We see this clearly in the bills that we get from utility firms that provide us with telephones, cell phones, electricity, and gas. Each bill provides a list of specific items where our precise usage is quantified, but for most of us the bill is basically incomprehensible. The documents preserve the fiction that we have bought a specific shopping cart full of specific services.

Moreover, with many of these items, there is an absence of transparency in their pricing systems. We see this now with airlines that use algorithms to constantly change the price of tickets for the same flight depending on shifts in demand, so it is entirely possible that each traveler has paid a different amount for their particular seat. Moreover, hidden fees or surprise fees are increasingly common in many service transactions. This is particularly a problem with financial services, but it is increasingly common at hotels and other tourist destinations.

The fundamental issue, however, is that destandarization effectively undermines the commensurability on which the market mechanism depends. For the market to equilibrate supply and demand, at least some shoppers are supposed to compare the relative cost of dinner given the prices that day for beef, chicken, and fish. However, product differentiation makes it extremely difficult to figure out whether a product with one set of bells and whistles is a better deal than one with a different set of bells and whistles. We used to face that difficulty only occasionally with big-ticket items like houses and cars, but now we face the dilemma of incommensurability for many consumer decisions.

Destandarization effectively shifts power from the consumer to the producer. Economists recognize that what they call "information asymmetries" are present in many market transactions. This means simply that producers have much more knowledge of their product than consumers, making it possible for producers to charge more than the product is worth. Destandardization effectively increases these information asymmetries. One of the few strategies available to consumers in this situation is to rely on brand names to protect themselves from bad purchases. This means, in turn, that markets can be dominated by a few large firms able to afford large advertising budgets. Consequently, it can be rational for firms to spend more money on advertising than on fixing defects in their products.

THE RISE OF THE SUBSCRIPTION MODEL

Another common feature of habitation economies has been the steady expansion of the subscription model of consumption. The shift of newspapers in the U.S. to a subscription model began in the depression of the 1930s. Prior to that, newspapers were hawked in the street by working-class newsboys. When big cities had multiple daily papers, a person could pick a different paper on each day of the week. For the person who buys a newspaper from one of those newsboys or from a newsstand, the paper is a classical commodity. However, taking out a subscription for a newspaper or another periodical establishes a longer-term relationship.

Many service sector relationships now follow the subscription model. Most people need mortgage loans to purchase their homes, so the monthly mortgage payment or the tenant's rent check can be thought of as a housing subscription. Utilities such as electricity, natural gas, water, sewerage, cable television, telephone, and cell phone are usually provided through contracts that involve monthly or bi-monthly bills. Similarly financial services such as banking, insurance, retirement accounts, and brokerage accounts operate as subscriptions. In healthcare, both health maintenance organizations and preferred provider plans work through annual enrollments and periodic billing. Admission to private schools or colleges and universities is essentially a fixed-term subscription where one pays a monthly, termly or annual fee until the degree is granted.

The rise of the subscription model has been accelerated by the widespread use of the personal computer. Software firms came to recognize that rather than issuing periodic upgrades of their popular software packages, revenues would be more predictable if they transformed consumers into subscribers who would pay an annual fee to access the most up-to-date version of the software. And with the development of the technology of streaming, subscriptions to one or another service is the only way to see the most popular entertainment products.

Moreover, since the start of the twenty-first century, there has been a significant increase in the transformation of consumer purchase of goods into subscriptions. Movement in this direction started as automotive companies and other producers of consumer goods offered customers extended warranty plans. The consumer paid an added fee to the producer or the retailer to be compensated for problems with the product that might occur in the future. The growth of automobile leasing was another step in this direction with 20 per cent of cars acquired this way in 2021. In fact, some automotive companies make more money on financing and leasing than from the production of cars.

The next step in the expansion of the subscription model is for firms to provide consumers with a contract to deliver home heating services, or air conditioning services, or solar panel services. In this model, the firm continues to own the equipment and is committed to replacing it when something goes wrong, and the customer pays a monthly subscription service.[4] While this business model is still in its infancy for retail customers, it is likely to grow substantially in coming years.

While it is easy to cancel the subscription to a newspaper when one is angered by an editorial or stop a streaming service when another one seems more attractive. But other subscriptions tend to lock the consumer into a long-term relationship where exit can be difficult, costly, or impossible. With many of the services that are classified as public utilities, a single firm has a monopoly that is supposed to be regulated by a public authority. However, the regulators in many cases have become captives of the regulated firms and are relatively insensitive to consumer concerns about rate increases or poor service.

Here again, the subscription model works to shift power from consumers to producers. Not only does exit become more difficult, but pricing tends to lack transparency, and providers have reduced incentives to maintain service quality. Moreover, many consumers have encountered the issues that come up with problems of interoperability. For example, when problems occur with watching a program on a particular streaming service, it can be difficult to figure out whether the problem lies with the streaming service, with the device attached to the television that facilitates streaming, with the television itself, with the wireless router, or with the modem linking the house to the internet. Help lines are likely to put the blame on one of the other providers.

THE COMMUNICATION/INFORMATION/ ENTERTAINMENT SYSTEM

It is not obvious from the official data, but a growing share of consumer dollars goes to pay for communication, information, and entertainment. Some of this is paid for directly through phone bills, cable television bills, internet fees, and ticket sales for concerts and sports events. However, much of it is paid for indirectly through advertising. For example, radio, broadcast television, many podcasts, and most of our access to social media are provided for free, but these services are paid for by advertising that is ultimately added to the cost of goods and services that we purchase. Estimates are that the total advertising outlays in the U.S. in recent years are close to $300 billion annually.

On the one side, these new communications or information platforms provide consumers with an almost infinite set of choices. The three national broadcast networks in the U.S. of the 1950s and 1960s have given way to hundreds of different channels on many cable or satellite television systems. Similarly, on Facebook and other social media, there is space for a vast differentiation of interest groups, including enthusiastic followers of some of history's most notorious mass murderers. Nevertheless, the explosion of individual choice masks the reality that we have collectively lost the ability to control what these services actually do.

We know now, for example, that the algorithms used on these platforms are designed to maximize user engagement in order to sell advertisers more consumer eyes. Since content that provokes strong emotion is likely to stimulate engagement, consumers are served with materials that will catch their attention and pull them into even further engagement. This is a formula for radicalization as when hundreds of thousands of people who were already sympathetic to Donald Trump were drawn into the more extreme views of Q-Anon or various white supremacist groupings. We also know that engagement with social media has negative consequences for adolescents whose anxieties about fitting in are intensified by the ubiquity of online rankings and bullying behavior.

The paradox could not be any more extreme. On the one side, the internet-based technologies have an amazing capacity to make knowledge available in ways that were previously unimaginable. People in remote parts of the world with internet access can sign up for online courses that connect them to the most up-to-date scientific knowledge available anywhere in the world. Yet the same technologies have effectively undermined the newspaper industry whose reporters had been the public's main source of information about what local and state elected officials were doing. The technologies also permit the more rapid diffusion of misinformation, dangerous rumors, and outright lies. Moreover, with advances in artificial intelligence and the rise of deep fakes, distinguishing between truth and falsehood is becoming increasingly difficult.

Finally, the extraordinary profits that a handful of global social media companies have been able to earn has effectively insulated them from effective regulation. The combination of campaign contributions and the ability to influence elections through manipulating the content that viewers see has made it difficult for elected officials to risk pushing for serious regulatory measures.

LIMITS ON GOVERNMENTAL EFFECTIVENESS

The argument, so far, is that in a habitation economy, consumers have limited opportunities to meet their needs through the market because most of what they consume are not the classical standardized commodities provided by multiple producers. The combination of destandardization, the subscription model, and growing concentration among providing firms has significantly reduced consumer leverage. Even where exit is a feasible move for the consumer, as is possible with insurance companies or cell phone carriers, the reality is that most firms are using similar algorithms and similar strategies to maximize profits. There is no guarantee that another company will have better service or more transparent pricing. In fact, one could easily end up with a worse provider.

One might think that in a situation where markets are failing, the government might step in and provide a regulatory framework that helped consumers get what they need. The reality, however, is that even though the public sector is heavily involved in many of these markets, existing political and budgetary constraints have meant that government at local, state, and federal levels have done very little to make providers more responsive to consumer needs. In fact, there are numerous cases where public agencies have made the problem of non-responsive providers even worse.

Let's start with the issue of housing. Government at all levels are heavily involved in the markets for both rental and owner-occupied housing. The federal government basically undergirds the housing market through government-sponsored enterprises such as Fannie Mae that purchases mortgages and resells them as mortgage-backed bonds. The total annual amount of real estate lending that is backed by the federal government exceeds the amount of new residential investment by business. Moreover, the government also subsidizes real estate development through extremely generous depreciation allowances that make it possible for developers to minimize taxes on their profits.

Local governments regulate the housing industry through building permits, planning permission, zoning laws, and the governance of landlord–tenant relations. Nevertheless, these formidable governmental powers have not been sufficient to increase the supply of affordable housing. On the contrary, the supply of affordable housing has been shrinking and increasing numbers of people face one or another of the consequences: substandard housing, very long commutes, spending more than 50 per cent of the household's income on housing, and homelessness.

There are multiple reasons for this failure. First, there has been a retreat from government provision of public housing. This was symbolized by the highly visible destruction of some of the Pruitt–Igoe public housing in St. Louis, Missouri in 1972. The high-rise complex was originally built in 1954 as part of urban renewal, but the concentration of low-income African-American families and poor maintenance practices transformed the complex into a haven for vandalism and crime. Efforts at reform failed and as vacancies increased, the city opted for demolition. The Nixon Administration used this failure to justify a moratorium on new public housing in 1974. Since then, government housing for the poor has focused on voucher programs that help low-income families afford rent, but such programs do not increase housing supply.[5]

States and cities generally lack the resources to finance the creation of new housing, and the firms that underwrite public debt offerings tend to be unsympathetic to bond offering to finance such housing. These investment bankers are more interested in financing projects that are likely to generate a future increase in local tax revenues that would help service the loan. The provision of housing for lower income residents hardly fits that particular calculation.

Another major factor in explaining why government powers have not been used to expand the supply of affordable housing is that real estate developers tend to have significant influence on local and state elected officials. Developers tend to be significant campaign donors since they want to be sure that they can get approval for their projects and in a good position to win public contracts. Moreover, the number of construction jobs is often a key element in the health of the local labor market, so politicians are usually anxious to retain the support of real estate interests. Reform coalitions sometimes win power at the local level, but they rarely retain power long enough to reverse the influence of real estate developers.[6]

One obvious example of the ongoing deference of local officials to real estate interests is the continuation of racially segregated housing patterns in much of the country. While the public policies that supported housing segregation have long since been dismantled, old racial boundary lines have often continued as real estate agents continue to steer clients to neighborhoods by race. These discriminatory practices could be stopped with vigorous enforcement, but few localities have invested the needed resources.

The story with other key elements of habitation is similar. The healthcare sector is strongly supported by federal spending for health insurance programs Medicare and Medicaid, and through billions for research at the National Institutes of Health. Physicians are licensed by states and hospitals are subject to multiple regulatory regimes. And yet there are extremely limited mechanisms to force the healthcare system to be responsive to the needs of citizens. When the HIV-AIDS epidemic was raging, it took a militant social movement to force the healthcare system to respond more aggressively with research and treatment for those with the disease.[7] A women's health movement has been pushing for decades to make the healthcare system more responsive to the specific health needs of half the population, but successes have been limited. To this day, for example, maternal mortality rates among African American women are two and a half times the rate for white women.[8]

Moreover, everyone has experience with healthcare providers or hospitals that routinely treat patients disrespectfully or subject them to unnecessary bureaucratic red tape. The message is routinely sent that the physician's time is extremely valuable, and the patient should be grateful no matter how long the wait. Moreover, it often takes years to remove a doctor who criminally abuses patients, so there is little chance that these more minor abuses will ever be remedied.

One of the most important symptoms of the unresponsiveness of the healthcare system is the crisis created by overprescribing opioids. Drug companies incentivized physicians to make use of these newly available drugs to manage patient pain, but the consequence was that hundreds of thousands of people became addicted. Death rates from drug overdoses soared and many lives were ruined. It took almost a decade before actions were taken to curb the use of opioids, but these restrictions intensified the problem as people who had become addicted shifted to heroin and other dangerous illegal drugs.

Another less dramatic but also important symptom is that millions of people have health problems that most medical providers either ignore or trivialize. This has fed the growth of a quite large alternative health sector that offers a range of therapies many of which are derived from non-Western traditions. While some people find significant relief through this sector, the fact that it is largely unregulated creates opportunities for predatory and potentially dangerous interventions.

Despite all these problems, almost nobody ever raises the idea that our healthcare system should be governed democratically. While it would make no sense to have people vote on which medicines to use against a pandemic or whether a particular patient should have a bypass operation. But given that we are collectively paying for the healthcare system and that the market mechanism provides very little leverage, would it not make sense to have the healthcare system in each locality overseen by a democratically elected board?

Such a board could collect citizen complaints about unresponsiveness and poor behavior by medical care providers. It could operate as an early warning system for problems like the over-prescribing of opioids or heightened levels of infant or maternal mortality. Most critically, it could provide a voice for the public at the table about healthcare priorities such as the distribution of resources between prevention and treatment. It could also provide direct input into local government about immediate threats to public health that require changes in public policy.

A parallel argument can be made about another key aspect of habitation: the transportation infrastructure that facilitates or blocks the ability of people to get from one place to another. Here again, much of this infrastructure has been directly funded by government, whether we are talking about roads and bridges, buses, subways, or light rail. However, the decisions about transportation spending were usually made by technocrats with relatively little public input.

As towns and cities cope with the simultaneous issues of climate resilience, shortage of affordable housing, and the clean energy transition, would it not make sense to give voters a greater voice in deciding what short-term and long-term improvements in the transportation infrastructure should be made? Here again, there is an obvious need for expert knowledge about transportation and budgeting. However, one can imagine a model where different citizen groups are given budgets to work with experts to develop competing transportation plans, and then some combination of citizen assemblies and referenda could be used to choose among the different plans.

CONCLUSION

In a habitation economy the most important forms of consumption are shared or collective. What matters for our quality of life are not the items that we can pull off a shelf at a big-box retailer, but the quality of the environment, of the neighborhood, of the housing, of the healthcare system, of the education system, of the energy infrastructure, of the transportation system, of the communication and information system, and so on. Markets are not an effective instrument for exerting control over these forms of shared consumption, and our political system has effectively blocked citizens from having effective input into how these systems are structured.

The further complexity is that with rising inequality of income and wealth, the problem is not just lack of control; it is that many people are excluded from minimally adequate forms of collective consumption. We see this most dramatically with increases in homelessness, and ever larger numbers of people dealing with unaffordable housing. It was also evident in the Covid pandemic where fatalities were higher in Black, Brown, and Native American communities where access to healthcare resources were limited. Moreover, in many neighborhoods, underfunded public schools occupy deteriorating buildings with demoralized and undertrained teaching staffs.

Some of our ongoing political debates center on these patterns of exclusion. The healthcare reform that President Obama carried through was designed to significantly reduce the percentage of the population without health insurance coverage. It did not address the problem of making the healthcare system more accountable to the people it serves. Similarly, advocates of school vouchers and charter schools argue that they want to upgrade educational opportunities for those who have been poorly served by the public school system. Advocates for the homeless push for localities to provide transitional housing to help the formerly homeless get reintegrated into society.

While protecting people from exclusion and marginalization is an urgent task, such efforts have a Sisyphean quality. As the shortage of affordable housing intensifies, for example, people receiving transitional housing will soon be replaced by newly evicted individuals and families. Getting people affordable health insurance does not solve their problems if they are still last in line at overcrowded and understaffed healthcare facilities. Inclusion policies will have limited effectiveness without significantly expanding the economic resources that localities are able to mobilize. Moreover, there is good reason to doubt that political support for expanding those economic resources can be mobilized if the focus is largely on helping those who are currently excluded and marginalized.

What follows from this analysis is a focus on creating habitation that is both democratic *and* inclusive. The two tasks have to be addressed at the same time; we need political and economic restructuring that gives all citizens greater control over their habitation while also prioritizing the needs of those who have been marginalized or excluded. The metaphor for this politics has been powerfully articulated by Heather McGhee—the drained public pool.[9] Back when courts started to outlaw overt discrimination against African Americans, many municipalities faced a dilemma. Should they allow public swimming pools to be racially integrated or would they just close them down? The latter option was chosen in many places with the consequence that children of *all* races who could not afford to join private swimming clubs lost out. The path forward is to rebuild those swimming pools and upgrade habitation for everyone.

4

The irony of corporate dominance

In the era of standardized commodities, a particular type of organization became the dominant type of business firm in the economy. This was the large multi-divisional, hierarchical corporation that excelled at producing large quantities of standardized items with great efficiency.[1] However, we continue to rely on this same type of organization to produce destandardized goods and services in a habitation economy even though other organizational models are actually better at producing destandardized goods and services. Since these organizations have very deep pockets and considerable influence in the political system, they have been able to continue their dominance despite the fact that other types of organization might be more effective and more efficient. Their continuing dominance is one of the key reasons why we are not able to have the kind of habitation that most of us would like to have.

The concept of monoculture that comes from farming provides a useful analogy. Critics of industrial-style agriculture employ the term to describe what happens when large areas of land are shifted from cultivating multiple types of vegetation to focusing on a single crop or one particular type of livestock. For farming organizations, monoculture often seems like an obvious and efficient choice since it allows for the optimal use of both farm machinery and land. Monoculture is basically the application of the assembly line to agricultural production to reduce the cost of production of each unit of output.

Critics point out, however, that the cost–benefit supporting monoculture is often misleading. Vast expanses of the same crop are an invitation to the rapid proliferation of pests and disease that specialize in that particular crop or species of animal. Furthermore, monoculture tends to deplete the soil of key nutrients requiring ever larger outlays for fertilizer which, in turn, has negative environmental consequences. Concentrated animal feeding operations such as giant pig farms produce huge lagoons of animal waste that can seep into the ground water and produce noxious odors for miles around. In sum, monoculture might be profitable in the short term, but it can be unsustainable and inefficient over the longer term.

The metaphor of monoculture applies to the non-agricultural economy when a single type of organization becomes the dominant model for the entire economy. This is the case with the large, vertically organized corporations that first emerged in the last decades of the nineteenth century. These organizations have always co-existed with many small and medium-sized businesses including family businesses. However, large corporations have been able to appropriate the greater share of profits because of their size and their economic power. One sees this in franchise arrangements where a large corporate organization works with a series of smaller businesses that have paid for the right to provide the company's products in a certain location. These franchisers are both a source of revenue, and they absorb many of the risks that the large firm would otherwise face. Even beyond franchising, there are many other small businesses that are heavily dependent on large firms including retailers who rely on Amazon's platform or developers of apps for smart phones.

The structural advantage of large corporations is exemplified by the familiar pattern where the big national pizza chain comes to town and drives the local pizzeria out of business by selling pizzas at heavily discounted price. The big firm's deep pockets allow it to absorb losses, but the small family-owned pizzeria cannot survive a prolonged period of diminished revenues. The losses can be recouped by increasing prices significantly as soon as the local competition has been eliminated. This pattern has been followed for multiple products and services. Fifty years ago, most pharmacies were small and locally owned, and this continues to be the case in most communities with fewer than 50,000 people.

However, in larger communities, these small firms have been replaced by a handful of big national chains that have been able to realize economies of scale by creating networks of thousands of stores. They use aggressive pricing strategies to accelerate the retirement of independent pharmacists.

More recently, this logic of consolidation has been pursued in local real estate offices, nursing homes, and other care facilities. Both for-profit and non-profit hospital chains in the U.S. are aggressively buying up physician's offices to consolidate control over the provision of health services in a geographical area. Moreover, some of these organizations operate networks of hospitals and medical practices that are national in scope.

As we shall see in a later chapter, this pattern of monocropping is supported by the structures of finance in the United States and the United Kingdom. In much of Western Europe, much of the financing for business firms has historically been provided by bank loans. This is a system that is friendly to small and medium-sized enterprises that have a track record of profitability. However, in the U.S. and the U.K. most corporate finance has been organized through the issuing of shares on stock markets. Banks, in recent decades, have not been active in financing business investment, except in real estate development where firms have substantial collateral that can be used to reduce the risks to bankers.

The stock market model of financing significantly reinforces the advantage of large hierarchical firms. The ambitious nursing home entrepreneur who buys up five or six other nursing homes is likely to be able to persuade investment bankers to float a stock offering that will provide the capital to buy up another ten facilities. Even if there are no economies of scale in creating a nursing home chain, as long as the accountants can show the firm to be profitable, more shares can be sold to finance further expansion. Growth through acquisition is a tried-and-true formula for creating ever larger firms, and the growth—by itself—can effectively postpone any questions about the effectiveness or ineffectiveness of the firm's management.

On the other side, the entrepreneur who wants to manage a firm without selling shares to the public faces serious obstacles to continued success. Finding capital to finance expansion will be difficult and will likely involve loans at high interest rates. There is a constant danger that an established larger firm might swoop in and provide a competing product at a lower price point or claim that the product infringes on its stockpile of thousands of patents. Moreover, in most contests to get favorable rulings or support from government entities, the larger firms will have an advantage because of their deeper pockets. Given the riskiness of continuing as an independent entity, many entrepreneurs in this situation end up accepting a buyout bid from an existing firm.[2]

In short, the monoculture of organizational forms is continuously being reproduced by the existing structures without any assessment of whether the large hierarchical firm remains the most productive or efficient way to do business. In a habitation economy organized around destandardized products, there is pressure on businesses to innovate continuously. But when we look closely at the innovation process, it becomes obvious that these large entrenched firms are actually not very good at innovating.

UBIQUITOUS INNOVATION

Innovation is at the center of the economy since firms that are not continuously adding new features risk losing market shares to their competitors. To be sure, much of the resulting innovation is superficial, fanciful, fraudulent, or even harmful.[3] Nevertheless, an ever-growing share of the economy is now devoted to producing more substantial innovations based on cutting-edge scientific and technological advances.

In the twentieth century, the laboratories established by large corporations were responsible for many of the most important innovations. As already mentioned, AT&T's Bell Labs played a particularly important role in some of the key developments that advanced both computerization and new communications technology. Bell Labs, however, was effectively insulated from competitive pressures because of AT&T's monopoly position in the economy, so the company could afford to run its laboratory more like that of a university than a corporation.[4] However, the corporate laboratories at General Electric, General Motors, DuPont, Boeing, and other defense contractors were responsible for numerous significant innovations.

However, in the twenty-first century, the reality is very different. A substantially smaller share of the innovations come from the laboratories of large firms. We can see this clearly in an analysis of the R&D 100 awards, a competition organized by the U.S. magazine *R&D World*. The competition recognizes key innovations that are available in actual commercial products. In 1971, the largest firms were responsible for 41 out of 100 of these awards. By 2006, that number had dropped steadily to 6 out of 100. The marginal role of large firms in the awards has continued down to the more recent competitions.[5]

It is common to attribute this decline in the importance of corporate laboratories to the growing emphasis on Wall Street of maximizing shareholder value. Since the price of corporate equities are strongly influenced by quarterly financial results, top managers have to be focused on producing good results in the short term.[6] However, investments in the corporate laboratory are unlikely to produce immediate results; most new technologies take years of development. Under these pressures, some large firms closed down their laboratories or downsized them significantly.

But managerial short-termism is only part of the explanation. The reality is that the effectiveness of these corporate laboratories had been declining, so their budgets would likely have been cut even without pressures to maximize shareholder value. The core problem is greater technological complexity at the innovation frontier. The complexity means that overcoming technological barriers increasingly requires multi-disciplinary teams that bring together scientists and engineers with five or even ten different types of specific expertise.

It is not feasible for corporations to try to assemble these large multi-disciplinary teams inside of a corporate laboratory. Even such fantastically rich firms as Microsoft and Amazon pursue innovations with outside partners. Part of the issue is the cost of hiring technologists from multiple disciplines and the other part is the difficulty of finding people with the specific type of expertise who actually want to work in a corporate laboratory. In an era of downsizing, such jobs are far less attractive than working in a government laboratory or a university that provides greater job security. Moreover, scientists and engineers have heard tales of people who worked for years on promising projects in a corporate laboratory only to discover that their initiative was abruptly canceled when top management decided to go in a different direction. One can see in the data that over the decades people with PhD degrees have migrated from large firms to small and medium-sized firms where the chances of bringing a project to fruition appear higher.

These multi-disciplinary teams are now assembled through inter-organizational collaborations. Even the largest corporations now collaborate with both small firms that have highly specialized expertise and with publicly-funded laboratories or research institutes. It is rarely acknowledged but the U.S. government has more than 300 different government laboratories, some of which operate multiple facilities. These laboratories have been under pressure for years to increase their work in support of private businesses and in any year, there are many thousand active collaborations in process. In addition, the government has funded more than 1,000 research institutes of varying sizes, most often located on university campuses, whose mission is to do collaborative work with industry. Moreover, the trend has been to increase the size of these institutes to assure that they can easily assemble the needed multi-disciplinary scientific teams. The bills passed by the U.S. Congress in 2022—the Chips and Science Act and the Inflation Reduction Act—created dozens of new additions to the population of large, specialized, research institutes.[7]

The typical pattern is that these government-created research institutes recruit corporate partners who often pay dues to help support the institute. In addition to bringing together the multi-disciplinary teams required to overcome a technological barrier, these institutes often facilitate ongoing collaborations among member firms. For example, a larger firm might find several smaller partners with highly specialized expertise who go on to help overcome the barriers to producing the new product at a reasonable price point.

A FOOTBALL INTERLUDE

It is easier to understand how the innovation process works by looking at a specific case that exemplifies the problem of innovating amid technological complexity. The helmet used in the American game of football represents a small-scale version of the process. The first helmets in the 1920s and 1930s had been made of leather. The plastic helmet was introduced in 1939 and for 70 years was improved only incrementally with more padding and more complex face guards. In fact, the same firms dominated the industry for most of that period. Things started to change, however, in 2007 when it became known that football players were being diagnosed with chronic traumatic encephalopathy (CTE), a degenerative brain disease resulting from repeated concussions.

Change, however, did not occur immediately. It was not until 2015 that the NFL and the Players Association began a testing program to identify how helmets protected or failed to protect against head injury. In 2019, the league finally launched a well-funded helmet challenge. In the first stage of the competition, firms were invited to enter prototypes for improved helmets. In the second stage, $1.37 million was allocated to 13 teams whose prototypes proved particularly promising. In the third stage, announced in October 2021, $1.5 million was allocated to three of the teams with the most promising entries. The three teams will use the award funds to move towards mass production of their new helmets, so they can be put into use by NFL teams as quickly as possible.

Unlike some prize competitions, the helmet challenge involved close collaboration between the competing teams and groups of experts assembled by the NFL. The challenge was launched at a three-day symposium attended by 300 technologists in November 2019, held at the America Makes Institute in Youngstown, Ohio. America Makes is a government-funded advanced manufacturing institute focused on 3D printing or additive manufacturing.[8]

The NFL recognized that producing a significantly improved football helmet requires combining expertise in neuroscience, mechanical engineering, materials science, sophisticated computer modeling, and probably several other disciplines. The participants at the initial symposium were given access to a finite element model—a system of differential equations—that shows how four existing helmets respond to different types of impact. The teams that had a chance at winning the competition would need to provide a similar finite element model of their own helmet to show how it outperforms other helmets.[9]

As it happened, each of the three winning teams was itself a consortium that combined academic researchers with businesses. One winner was a Montreal-based collaboration called Kollide that brought together researchers from the engineering school at the University of Quebec with four firms with expertise in simulation, design, 3D printing, and software developed for three-dimensional body scans. A second winner was a start-up firm in Denver, Impressio, that was created in a partnership with the University of Denver. The third was a firm called Xenith, founded in 2006, that was already a helmet provider for the NFL. For its new helmet entry, Xenith worked in collaboration with RHEON Labs in London, a start-up firm that has developed a unique polymer, BASF, a major German chemical firm, and researchers at the University of Waterloo in Canada.

Developing an improved football helmet is typical of contemporary innovation across many industries; it requires the participation of entities with five, six, or even more types of scientific or engineering expertise. Moreover, the example also points to the danger to long-established firms. Their failure to innovate can lead to the sudden loss of markets that they have dominated for more than 50 years. However, the case is atypical in that the dollar amounts that the NFL has spent have been comparatively modest. Many of the other contemporary technology challenges require billions of dollars of investment in both R&D and in production facilities. This is true of the development of new generations of computer chips, advanced batteries for electric vehicles, new composite materials for construction, new vaccines and other biopharmaceuticals, and more sophisticated systems for 3D printing as an industrial tool.

In all of these cases, there is the need for multiple types of scientific and engineering expertise and very large investments. What the football helmet case demonstrates is that in innovation, the monoculture of large hierarchical firms is being replaced by what can be called "cooperative network production". Precisely because overcoming technological barriers requires multiple different types of expertise, interorganizational collaborations become indispensable. Moreover, we also see that collaborations between for-profit firms work best when there is a neutral third party involved in the network. In the football helmet case, the NFL played this role by providing the monetary incentives that made it much easier to hold together the different collaborative teams that entered the competition. In most cases, however, it is government personnel who play a key coordinating role in making cooperative network production work effectively.

THE THIRD-PARTY ROLE

The importance of this third-party role in cooperative network production has been explained by Andrew Schrank and Josh Whitford. They argue that as interorganizational collaborations increase in importance, network failure became a significant danger.[10] Firms often fail to find partners that are both trustworthy and have the necessary skills required for effective collaboration. Moreover, searching for partners is time consuming and costly especially when the ideal partner might be a small, recently launched startup. These searches occur in a context where the pressure on firms to maximize profits can lead them to deceive or even cheat a prospective partner. One firm can follow the strategy of "fake it until you make it" by claiming expertise that it does not yet have. Another firm might literally steal the intellectual property of the other or negotiate a contract that will unequally divide the profits from the collaboration. While that is usually done by the larger firm, a young Bill Gates negotiated a contract with IBM for the operating system of that company's first personal computer that resulted in Microsoft eventually overtaking IBM.

The neutral third party can significantly diminish these negative outcomes in a variety of different ways. Sometimes the third party can accelerate the process of finding needed network partners by drawing on its own network of connections. With government-sponsored research institutes, part of the goal is to recruit both large and small firms that have the greatest stake in a particular technology, so that collaborations will emerge spontaneously among member firms.

The third party also often has sufficient knowledge of the domain area to evaluate whether a potential partner has the competence that they claim to have.

The neutral third party can also operate as an honest broker to minimize opportunistic or exploitative behaviors between partners. For example, as part of the Manufacturing Extension Program (MEP) in the U.S., which is designed to upgrade the capacity of small manufacturing firms that produce parts for larger firms, the MEP consultants sometimes help firms negotiate better contracts with the original equipment manufacturers.[11] Similarly, the Small Business Innovation Research program (SBIR) in the Defense Department, which connects its firms with large defense contractors, protects the intellectual property of the smaller firms by using the SBIR application materials as being equivalent to a patent application. The large firms face sanctions if they copy the intellectual property without compensation.

However, the network failure framework does not exhaust the benefits of having a third party involved in these networked collaborations. Where the third party is well-funded, it can invest in equipment that significantly reduces costs for network participants. The Lawrence Berkeley National Laboratory constructed a small building mounted on a rotating table in order to test how well various energy-saving technologies worked when the sun was at different angles. Other institutes are building "test beds" or model manufacturing lines to help firms master the technologies required for advanced manufacturing. Earlier, the National Nanotechnology Initiative built a national network of nanotechnology laboratories that firms could use to run experiments or copy to build their own facilities.

Another important investment that the third party can make is in training the workforce that might be needed to develop innovations or to move them to large-scale production. In the network of advanced manufacturing institutes that were initially developed in the U.S. by the Obama Administration, quite a few of the institutes have developed curricula for local community colleges so they can provide prospective employees with the knowledge and skills needed to ramp up production. The paradigmatic historical example is that the U.S. Defense Advanced Research Projects Agency (DARPA) funded the creation of computer science departments at major universities in the U.S. in the early 1960s to create the initial pool of experts that was needed to accelerate the development of both hardware and software.[12]

Finally, the third party can also produce other public goods that other network participants are less able to provide. One example is the development of shared road maps. With cutting-edge technologies, all of the firms involved face a high level of uncertainty in developing strategies for rolling out risky new investments. Moving too slowly can mean lagging behind competitors and potentially losing markets. Moving too quickly can leave one with production capacity that cannot be used until others in the network catch up. Third parties can talk to all of the market participants and develop a consensual road map that includes timelines. While risks obviously remain, the shared road map facilitates coordination among different actors.

BEYOND INNOVATION

So far, the focus has been on the innovation process, but the argument is that cooperative network production is also increasingly becoming the model for the production of most goods and services. Once we start looking for it, we can see it in many different corners of the economy. Some manifestations can be quite exploitative and many lack the presence of an effective third party who can discourage predatory practices.

For many people the outsourcing of technologically unsophisticated products such as garments, athletic shoes and machine parts to overseas sweatshops or *Maquiladoras* on the Mexican border first signalled that production was no longer occurring in one firm. The design function would continue at corporate headquarters but all of the production work was carried out by subcontractors overseas. The logic was simply to take advantage of lower labor costs abroad. However, as products become more complex, we are seeing a parallel process in which firms come to depend on the specialized expertise of other firms to manufacture both parts and final products.

In the automotive industry, for example, we have seen a dramatic move away from Henry Ford's vision of producing steel, glass, and finished vehicles in the same complex. In the U.S. car industry today, two-thirds of the parts are provided by subcontracting firms that are then assembled together by the companies.[13] U.S. firms learned from the Japanese that in a context where the firm is producing many different models that are subject to ongoing changes, there are big efficiency gains in relying on specialist firms to produce a shifting array of products that are delivered "just in time" for final assembly.[14]

However, with the rise of automation, robotics, 3D printing, and other advanced manufacturing techniques, it is increasingly common for firms to rely on contract manufacturers with domain expertise to manage the entire production process. In fact, it is now possible to have virtual firms that could potentially earn billions in revenue with only a tiny staff at headquarters and each of the different corporate functions carried out by a different partner firm, including manufacturing, marketing, and delivery to customers.

In the entertainment industry and in the service economy, there are also many examples of cooperative network production. In Hollywood movies, for example, the production is organized through the collaboration of many highly specialized firms that represent the actors, the director, the film editors, the sound engineers, the lighting experts, and so forth. The studio or production company enters the process at the end to make the deals to market the movie to consumers.

Financial deals such as offerings of new stocks or bonds or loans for large real estate developments are often organized through a syndicate of investment banks and brokerage firms who each take responsibility for a share of the overall deal.

Healthcare in the U.S. is generally delivered as a cooperative endeavor among independent practitioners, group practices, hospitals, and a variety of specialized health organizations such as rehab hospitals and dialysis centers. It may require the patient to have strong advocates to produce effective communication among these different parties, but the diversified structure recognizes that different types of expertise have to be brought together to provide effective care.

In the case of higher education, most instruction occurs within a single organizational entity, but the different departments and schools usually retain a much higher level of autonomy than is typical for corporations or even other large non-profit organizations. Moreover, individual faculty are often seen as academic entrepreneurs who manage laboratories, apply for grants, have considerable authority over graduate students and post-docs, and sometimes even lead their own firms.

But while we can see cooperative network production in many different parts of the economy, the large vertical organizations of the industrial era continue their dominance. They are still able to command the bulk of the profits and their top executives are able to command wildly disproportionate rewards for their work. This is the driving force behind rising inequality of income and wealth. But their dominance also prevents society from realizing many of the potential benefits of new technologies. Corporate power frequently tilts the innovation process in directions that produce both profits and negative social consequences. Finally, corporate power blocks people from using their collective voice to demand the kinds of habitation that could actually meet their needs.

HOW THE CONFLICTS PLAY OUT

This conflict between two types of productive organization is played out continually in the pharmaceutical industry. The big pharma companies still maintain laboratories, but those laboratories rarely develop new drugs. Their major activity is to develop variants of existing drugs that are in danger of losing patent protection. They make relatively small changes in the formula for a drug, and then apply for a new set of patents that will protect the product from competition for another 20 years.

The reality is that almost all of the effective new medications emerge out of cooperative network production. Scientists at universities might develop a new molecule and work with a startup or one of the smaller pharmaceutical firms to explore the new drug's potential efficacy. But once they are convinced of the new drug's potential, they face a significant barrier. The clinical trials required to gain the Food and Drug Administration (FDA) approval of a new medication for the U.S. market can take several years and can cost anywhere from $15 million to $150 million.[15] Since this is a large expenditure for a small firm to finance, the usual pattern is that the smaller firm negotiates an agreement with one of the big pharma firms to finance the clinical trials. These deals usually also entrust the larger firm to market the drug through its already existing network of salespeople who maintain ongoing contacts with physicians. The consequence is that the bigger firm sets the price for the drug and holds on to a larger share of the profits.

In short, the productive work being done through cooperative network production ends up making the entrenched pharmaceutical firms even richer and more powerful. But the large firms are only willing to finance the clinical trials if a drug has the potential to produce substantial profits. This means that some potentially useful drugs simply sit on the shelf in a laboratory because no one was willing or able to pay for the trials. In response to this dysfunction, Congress in 1983 passed an orphan drug law that provided added incentives for firms to develop drugs for conditions that were uncommon. While this produced a number of useful and effective treatments, some of these orphan drugs end up being priced at tens of thousands of dollars for a monthly dose. In fact, some of the orphan drugs have become key profit centers for the pharmaceutical firms. Here again, the big pharmaceutical firms have enough clout in Congress to block most measures that would limit their profitability.

If the big pharma firms could be displaced from their control over the clinical trials, cooperative network production would likely produce a much more substantial pipeline of new drugs each year. Breaking this bottleneck might also generate more research into common conditions such as digestive disorders where there has been little progress in recent decades. Moreover, with a greater number of small and medium-sized firms in the drug marketplace, there would be increased competition and an improved likelihood that prices to consumers would start to fall.

One way to displace big pharma from running the clinical trials would be for a public agency to organize the clinical trials in cooperation with the major medical centers. This would have the substantial advantage of connecting drug trials more closely to clinical practice, so that problems with a potential drug could be identified more quickly. Moreover, having a neutral party in charge of the evaluation process would eliminate the risks in the current system that firms are cooking the data in various ways to improve the chances of winning FDA approval.

We can see an analogous conflict between the two organizational forms with internet platform firms. On the one side, these platforms enable cooperative network production since small entrepreneurs are able to gain access to huge numbers of consumers that previously would have necessitated vast outlays for advertising. On the other, a firm like Amazon is able to impose various fees on these third-party retailers leading to a finding that Amazon's profit margin on third-party sales was 20 per cent as compared to only 5 per cent on its own products.[16] Moreover, the more dependent these third-party retailers are on their sales on the Amazon platform, Amazon is empowered to extract an even larger share of the profits. We see similar dynamics with the ride-sharing services such as Uber and Lyft that represent yet another form of cooperative network production. When these services began, the drivers were able to keep 80 per cent of the revenue from users. However, once the service has gained market share and drivers have become dependent on the revenue, the company can change the formula, add extra fees, and incrementally reduce the revenue that drivers keep.

Similar to the innovation process, cooperative network production works best with the active involvement of a neutral party who can restrain and discourage predatory behavior. An interesting example of this comes from the case of cloud computing that is dominated by a handful of giant firms. The effective provision of these cloud computing services to other customers depends on continuous innovations in software development. However, much of the software that is being developed to help firms make optimal use of their stored data on the cloud is open-source software that is being continuously advanced by communities of programmers who are both self-employed and working for other firms. This is another manifestation of cooperative network production.

Researchers investigating cloud computing found that Amazon Web Services has a pattern of appropriating open-source advances and incorporating them into their system, while Google Cloud Platform has worked out a collaborative relationship with the open-source developers. Several non-profit foundations built to support open-source software play an active role in maintaining the integrity of the software systems and in encouraging respectful relations between Google and smaller firms. They conclude that this collaborative model facilitates much more rapid advances than Amazon's more proprietary approach.[17]

THE PERSISTENCE OF TAYLORISM

The entrenchment of large, hierarchical organizations has another deeply destructive consequence; it systematically disempowers the employees whose knowledge, creativity, and problem-solving skills are needed to make these firms productive and effective. The kind of hierarchical structures that existed for standardized production in the industrial era have remained in place even though firms are now producing destandardized goods and services and prioritizing innovation. While some firms employ workarounds that seek to incentivize employees and to improve organizational decision making, these fall far short of what could be accomplished with a different structure that actually empowered employees.

While the terminology is no longer in wide usage, the basic patterns of Taylorist or Fordist management continue down to the present day.[18] All of the important decisions about firm strategy remain concentrated in the hands of a small group of top managers. Even the employees with high levels of domain expertise rarely have a seat at the table when such decisions are made, even when the immediate choices have to do with different technological paths. The guiding idea is that top managers make the important decisions and everyone else in the firm should simply be implementing the chosen strategies.

This hierarchical structure is reinforced by the reality that most employment in the U.S. continues to be "at will", meaning that the employer has the right to fire employees even if they have been performing their tasks flawlessly. The only limitation is if employees can prove that the firing was the result of some kind of racial, gender or age discrimination, or retribution for reporting inappropriate behavior to government regulators. While high-level employees and those working under a union contract are usually protected from firing for no cause, top managers still have substantial opportunities to justify termination. Moreover, union contracts cover only a small share of private sector employees.

For a long time, employees at firms such as Google, Facebook, and Microsoft were envied for the perks that came with these jobs such as luxury buses to transport them to work, gourmet meals, and free exercise classes. However, when the post-Covid retrenchment occurred in 2023, many of these once-envied workers found out that they were also at-will employees who could be laid off in the thousands. At the same time, these firms began cutting back on some of those perks for the employees who remained.

Another key element of the devaluation of employees is the persistence of the legal doctrine in both the U.S. and the U.K. that the employing firm owns any work done by the employee while on payroll. Legal scholars have shown that this was not the legal regime in the nineteenth century; employees had rights in things they invented while working for someone else.[19] But with the rise of the large corporation, courts consistently ruled that employees had no such rights. If an employer can prove that a former employee who has gone on to create a new firm developed the idea for a new product while under employment, the innovator can be sued for stealing the employer's intellectual property.

On the one side, this doctrine provides employees with a powerful incentive to be secretive when they depart and start a new firm to pursue an innovative idea. However, it obviously reduces the incentive to come up with creative ideas at the workplace since someone else is likely to reap the benefits of one's ingenuity. Although firms use workarounds such as bonuses, promotions, stock options, and special recognition to encourage employees to be creative, all of these measures fall short of giving the employee an actual economic stake in the innovation.

This is certainly one reason that scientists and engineers with PhD degrees have voted with their feet. Forty years ago, most of the PhD scientists and engineers working for corporations worked at large firms, those with 10,000 or more employees. Now, however, they are more likely to work at small firms with 1,000 or fewer employees. This change is a big part of the transition to cooperative network production. This shift has to do with three factors. First, the risk is much greater that a project one has been working on for years will be abruptly canceled at a big firm where top managers choose a small number of new products to launch each year. Second, at the small and medium-sized firms, technologists are likely to have direct access to the firm's decision makers. Third, the innovators in a small company are likely to have a substantially larger financial stake in a successful innovation since they are often given equity as part of their compensation.

But the most important indicator of the persistence of Taylorism is how frequently employers adopt managerial strategies that rely on poorly trained, easily replaced, poorly compensated, or heavily monitored employees. This has clearly been a key element in the movement of manufacturing jobs to cheap labor countries overseas. We also see it domestically when employers contract with outside firms to supply them with "temp workers" who perform tasks without benefits and with minimal prospects for durable employment. It is also characteristic of the gig economy where employees are often both poorly paid and subjected to elaborate computerized monitoring.

There has also been increasing attention to the "ghost workers" who are often part of high-tech industries. When firms launch new products, it is common to have done only limited testing on how they will work in the hands of consumers. Firms then direct customers to contracted call centers where low-wage employees with simplified scripts try to help consumers make the products work.[20] The firm then presumably uses the data from the call center to make fixes that reduce the number of distressed customers.

This persistent Taylorist mindset rests on two fundamental assumptions. First, top managers always know best; their prestigious MBA's from top schools equip them to see the big picture and make the right decisions. Second, the soundest business strategy is always to reduce the amount one spends on employees. This is the logic behind periodic waves of corporate downsizing and the constant search for ways to take advantage of cheaper labor.

But however deeply entrenched these ideas are, they are counterproductive in a habitation economy for a multitude of different reasons. One of the most obvious was revealed during the Covid pandemic when it became apparent that shifting production overseas to take advantage of cheap labor resulted in acute shortages of many of the supplies needed to bolster public health. High-quality face masks, other personal protective equipment, as well as a variety of medications were suddenly in short supply because we had become dependent on supplies from China. In some cases, China reduced its exports, and in other cases, the disease slowed the loading and movement of the container ships that cross the Pacific. This produced the pervasive "supply chain" disruptions that led to shortages across much of the economy.

Even before Covid-19, researchers had demonstrated the importance for firms of carrying out manufacturing in the same place where they do research and development especially when the products being made are complex or dependent on sophisticated technologies.[21] One reason is that moving to mass production is really the final stage of R&D and the people who have developed the technology can play an important role in solving manufacturing problems. Moreover, it is useful when contemplating changes in the product to directly engage with the people who will have to manufacture it.

The other issue is the difficulty of keeping control of intellectual property, especially when production is carried out in China. There have been numerous cases where cutting-edge products manufactured in China by U.S. or European firms were successfully copied by Chinese firms. Sometimes this happens through Chinese requirements that intellectual property is shared as a precondition for allowing the investment, and sometimes it happens through industrial espionage. Recently, China has become the global leader in the production of advanced batteries for automobiles, but the battery technologies they have used were initially developed in the U.S.

But the most important point is that this generalized disempowering of employees systematically undermines the production of habitation. Doctors who are limited to 15 minutes with each patient and nurses with too high caseloads are unable to provide quality healthcare. Other care workers who are underpaid and exploited cannot be expected to consistently provide kind and respectful treatment of their clients. Delivery people subject to intense control of their worktime are more likely to leave packages at the wrong address. Public sector employees, from teachers to social workers to bus drivers to building inspectors, who are disrespected by their supervisors are more likely to mistreat those they are supposed to be helping.

THE FORGOTTEN BENEFITS OF FLATTER ORGANIZATIONS

Back in the 1970s and 1980s when Silicon Valley was relatively young, much was written about how the new generation of technology firms had much flatter organizational structures than the hierarchies of established firms including the big three automotive companies, General Electric, and even IBM. Flatter firms meant fewer layers of management between the people who were developing new technologies and the top managers who were making decisions about the firm's priorities in terms of product development and investment.

With flatter organizations, there could be more direct communication between the key technologists and the relevant top managers. Instead of communication in each direction being mediated through multiple layers of middle management with the potential for distortion or the omission of key data, direct communication helps keep top managers better informed and the technologists can also feel that they are being heard.

Moreover, the flatter structure also gives the technologists a better chance to make the case for a new product or process. The people working at the Xerox Parc Laboratory in Palo Alto developed many of the technologies that were critical for the personal computer such as the mouse and the graphical user interface, but they were unable to persuade top managers at Xerox that the company should try to sell a personal computer.[22] It was that weakness in hierarchical organizations that made it possible for people in their early 20s like Steve Jobs and Bill Gates to build entirely new corporate empires.

The irony, of course, is that Apple and Microsoft, as well as later technology innovators such as Google (Alphabet), Facebook (Meta), and Amazon have grown up to be the same kind of steep hierarchies that they had vowed to replace. This was a more or less inevitable consequence of the enormous growth in the scope of their operations as well as the aggressive acquisition of other firms. With Apple's worldwide employment of more than 160,000 people, it becomes impossible to do without all of those intervening levels of management to coordinate the activities of that many people.

At the same time, we can see in coordinated network production, the continued advantages of flatter organizations. As mentioned earlier, many of the key pharmaceutical breakthroughs of the past 20 years have come from biotech firms where relatively small groups of technologists work together intensively to develop new medications. In fact, some of the classic descriptions of the innovation process focus on the mobilization of collective spirit and enthusiasm in groups working together to make a new product. Tracy Kidder tracked a group at the now defunct computer firm Data General as they worked to produce a new microcomputer that launched in 1980.[23] Richard Lester and Michael Piore provide an account of several episodes in which two groups with different expertise come together, gradually develop a common language, and then the team spirit required to overcome the barriers to genuine innovation.[24]

In fact, one of the paradigmatic moments in modern technology demonstrates the advantage of small and flat over large and hierarchical. IBM, the dominant firm in the computer industry, recognized belatedly that there was a mass market for the personal computer as Apple and other pioneering firms were racking up significant sales. However, instead of using its existing organizational structure to create IBM's first personal computer, the company instead imitated what a startup would do. They assembled a team and located them at a facility in Boca Raton, Florida that was kept isolated from other parts of the organization, relying on the team spirit and creativity of a face-to-face group to develop the machinery that remains the model for much of the personal computer industry. This strategy cut the development time from IBM's usual five years to one year, and allowed the team to violate a range of standard IBM practices.

While the team strategy worked with the hardware, the same did not happen with the operating system. As mentioned earlier, when IBM managers negotiated with a young Bill Gates to provide the operating system, he insisted that Microsoft retain ownership rights in the operating system. Managers from IBM's hierarchy failed to recognize that software was the future and they accepted Gates's terms. The consequence was that Microsoft was ultimately able to surpass IBM in size and market capitalization.

Yet another advantage of flatter organizations is that they are usually better able to work cooperatively with other entities. The whole basis of cooperative network production is that such cooperation is necessary because even the largest firms lack all of the needed expertise. However, in the big, hierarchical firms, top managers are under constant pressure to maximize shareholder value. This means that they cannot let sentiment get in the way; they often have to make hard decisions that negatively impact their employees, their subcontractors, their customers, or their corporate partners.

This pattern is clear with original equipment manufacturers such as automotive companies that subcontract with other firms to produce some of the critical parts used in their vehicles. Middle managers who oversee these relations have learned the lessons of Japanese lean production and have sought to build cooperative relations with these subcontractors. Cooperation means that the larger firm is loyal to the subcontractor, and the subcontractor, in turn, is innovating, keeping costs down, and facilitating changes in the specification of particular parts. Periodically, however, higher level managers decide that parts are costing too much and they insist that all subcontractors be required to cut prices by 10 per cent. Such edicts obviously interfere with the cooperative relationship and middle managers are left to try to patch things up with the subcontracting firm.

Similarly, a scientist or engineer working collaboratively with another entity will have to get clearance from multiple levels of managers to share a particular piece of intellectual property with others while the counterpart at a flatter organization will have direct access to the key decision maker. In all these cases, hierarchy gets in the way of establishing mutual trust with people outside the organization. And diminished levels of mutual trust are likely to interfere with effective interorganizational collaborations.

CONCLUSION

Our economy is still dominated by dinosaurs: the giant hierarchical organizations that came to dominate in the industrial era when mass production involved many huge factories employing tens of thousands of workers. Those firms were successful because they were able to take advantage of economies of scale and scope. However, this has long since ceased to be the reality. In today's economy with its emphasis on innovation, destandarization, and continuous technological advances, the remaining large corporations have increasingly become dependent on networks of cooperating firms both for innovation and for production.

However, since these corporate dinosaurs are protected by the existing financial structures and their considerable sway in the political system, they have refused to die off. In fact, the tech industry has given birth to a whole new species of corporate dinosaurs that have made people like Musk, Bezos and Zuckerberg fantastically wealthy. While the real dynamism in the economy comes from the emergent structures of cooperative network production, in case after case, the dinosaurs have figured out ways to gobble up a disproportionate share of the profits that cooperative network production makes possible. They have then been able to recycle a portion of those profits into political interventions designed to further entrench their positions.

At the same time, the dinosaurs are also blocking the significant potential that cooperative network production has to improve habitation. We saw with drug development that the established drug firms take advantage of the clinical trial bottleneck to limit their investments to a handful of new drugs with the potential to be billion-dollar blockbusters. At the height of the Covid pandemic when ventilators were in short supply, the *New York Times* reported that the federal government had years earlier contracted with a small startup to develop a substantially cheaper ventilator. However, before that firm could deliver on the contract, it was purchased by a competitor that produced more expensive ventilators and that had no interest in fulfilling the contract to provide ventilators at a substantially lower price point.[25]

We have no data on how common it is for bigger firms to buy up competitors to kill off their innovations. But the number of acquisitions in Silicon Valley is so large that some of them are likely to fall into this category. Facebook has acquired more than 97 companies, Microsoft has purchased more than 270 companies, and Google/Alphabet has bought more than 250.[26] At the very least, this frenzied pace of acquisitions can be seen as a conscious effort to minimize the possibility that cooperative network production based on hundreds or even thousands of small and medium-sized enterprises will take root in Silicon Valley.

At the same time, the tech dinosaurs have been able to use their deep pockets and the political clout that follows from the wealth of their billionaire owners to block any effective government regulation of their often-destructive practices. Their role in spreading misinformation, fomenting political polarization, invading privacy, and undermining the mental health of young people is now well documented. Now, we face destructive social consequences from the unleashing of new generations of artificial intelligence. While the need for an effective system of regulation seems obvious, it has not yet emerged.

In the counterfactual, where these technologies would have emerged under a regime of cooperative network production, effective regulation would have emerged much more organically. The public sector role in helping reduce network failures could have been extended into providing guidelines for industry best practices that could have avoided some of the abuses that have now become industry standards. Moreover, with profits divided across many different firms, the fantastic profits that allow the dinosaurs to block effective regulation would not be concentrated in a small number of hands.

5

What counts as investment?

There are two powerful mechanisms that work to entrench the dominance of hierarchical corporations. Chapter 6 will explain how our current financial system reinforces corporate dominance and helps to keep people from exercising control over their habitation. This chapter explains how the categories of mainstream economics produce a systematic mismeasurement of the amount of investment in the economy. This mismeasurement, in turn, reinforces the idea that public policy should be oriented towards incentivizing business investment. This leads directly to limitations on both public spending and wage gains for workers since both of these come at the expense of corporation profitability. The consequence is a systematic underinvestment in the expenditures that would improve our habitation.

Even though we have a habitation economy, we are using the economic tools that were developed to understand an industrial economy. Among the most important of these tools are the definition of investment and the accounting methods for measuring it. Investment is generally defined by economists as the production of goods that will be used to make other goods.[1] Whether or not an outlay is defined as an investment has important consequences for measuring total output.

Investment outlays are contrasted with spending on intermediate goods that are used up in the process of production, such as the steel and glass used to make automobiles or a company's use of bookkeeping services. These intermediate goods are not included in GDP since their cost is incorporated in the price of final products. Investment is also distinguished from consumption activity that simply uses up the supply of goods and services produced in a given year. It follows that when an expense that was previously defined as either an intermediate good or a consumption good is redefined as an investment, it increases gross domestic product (GDP). GDP is the sum of investment *plus* the total amount of goods and services that are consumed by final users *plus* government spending *plus* the balance of international trade.[2] In short, investment expenditures are productive whereas consumption simply uses up what has been produced elsewhere; intermediate goods are necessary but do not have the generative power of investments.

Every economic paradigm makes its own distinction between productive and unproductive activities. The Physiocrats—eighteenth-century precursors to modern economists—insisted that only agriculture was productive and both commerce and industry simply used up resources produced by agriculture.[3] Housewives were coded as productive early in the nineteenth century but were defined as unproductive by the end of the century.[4] Through most of the nineteenth century, economists defined banking activity as unproductive, but in the second half of the twentieth century, it was redefined as productive.[5] It follows that disagreements about the proper operationalization of the investment category are, in fact, arguments about what is productive and what is not productive.

Over the twentieth century, economic transformations have created problems for mainstream economics in how it constructs and justifies its definition of investment. There has been an accumulation of what Thomas Kuhn referred to as anomalies in the paradigm, as different economists have proposed significantly different measures of investment and the government agency in the U.S. responsible for the national income accounts has not been able to align its concept of investment with the views of most economists.[6] Since 1996, the Bureau of Economic Analysis (BEA) in the Department of Commerce has made a series of revisions in its definition of investment. However, these changes have not resulted in a measurement scheme that is theoretically coherent.

The argument here is that both mainstream economists and the BEA are working with inadequate schemes for measuring the total amount of investment in the economy. Moreover, the same inadequacies plague the measurement of GDP across all of the developed market economies. The inability of statistical agencies to develop and implement a theoretically coherent measurement scheme suggests an urgent need for a different paradigm that defines investment in a more consistent and coherent way. The foundation for this alternative paradigm has already been constructed by two different group of analysts. The first are feminist theorists of social reproduction and the second are scholars who have argued that significant parts of social welfare spending can be reconceptualized as social investment. The contribution of this chapter is to use data from the U.S. national income accounts and other sources to show how this alternative paradigm facilitates a more persuasive account of what activities are productive and what are not. This exercise revises our understanding of the relative role of business, government, households, and non-profits in the economy. Moreover, it calls into question the familiar arguments in favor of austerity policies that have exerted extraordinary influence over the past four or five decades. Those austerity policies have been critical in keeping us from creating the kind of habitation that most people would want.

The data for this study are drawn from the United States, but the argument is relevant to other developed market societies as well as to developing nations that have moved beyond an economy dominated by the production of raw materials. However, the empirical results would be even more dramatic for many European nations where social spending programs are considerably more generous than in the United States.

OFFICIAL MEASURES OF INVESTMENT

Debates about the boundary line between productive and unproductive expenditures go back centuries, but we will start with the development of national income accounting in the U.S. and the U.K. in the 1930s and 1940s. In those decades, a very large percentage of the labor force were working on farms or in factories producing tangible products that were loaded on trains and trucks to be delivered to consumers. That economy was very different from today's, which is dominated by the service sector and where fewer than 10 per cent of employees work in factories or on farms. In that earlier period, it was common sense to define investment narrowly as private expenditures on tangible items such as buildings, machinery, and vehicles. This was the operationalization used in the first U.S. national income accounts published by the BEA in 1947.

Complexities of measuring investment

Before reviewing how this definition changed over time, it is important to look more closely at several of the complexities of the investment category. First, the decision to code something as an investment is independent of the actual outcome. People, for example, routinely spend large sums of money to remodel and equip retail stores or restaurants that fail within six months. This expenditure still counts as investment in the national income accounts even though it ultimately proved to be unproductive. Similarly, in boom periods, businesses commonly produce too many office buildings or houses or lay too much fiber optic cable. This counts as investment since resources have been diverted from consumption. In short, the definition of investment does not require that the expenditures are *actually* productive or that they earn some particular rate of return. The point is simply that the expenditures have the potential to increase economic output over time.

Second, analysts distinguish gross investment from net investment. Net investment is equal to gross investment minus depreciation or capital consumption. Investment goods such as buildings, machinery, and vehicles will deteriorate over time and eventually become obsolete so some portion of gross investment is simply offsetting or compensating for this deterioration. In theory, only net investment—what is left after depreciation is subtracted—is actually increasing the economy's total productive capacity. While this distinction makes sense, operationalizing the concept of capital consumption is fiendishly complex. To avoid this complexity, this chapter will focus on gross investment flows.[7]

However, we shall return later to the issue of how depreciation is calculated for different types of investment.

A third big issue involves the relationship between measurements of investment and the conceptualization of capital or the total stock of productive assets. While some recent scholarship has focused on refining conceptions of capital, most of it does not address the complicated issues of measuring investment flows. In his influential book, *Capital in the Twenty-First Century*, Thomas Piketty devotes only a few pages to defining capital. He states that domestic capital includes the land, infrastructure, machinery, computers, and patents owned by government and business firms,[8] but he does not probe more deeply into which specific assets belong in the investment category.

Other recent scholars have broadened the concept of capital beyond land, buildings, and machinery to include human capital, cultural capital, and social capital. However, it seems that neither cultural capital nor social capital are produced through investments that can be quantified in dollar terms. Cultural capital appears to be created as a byproduct of socialization in the family and social capital can be produced through almost any activity that constructs social ties.[9] It has been suggested, for example, that connections formed when Chinese young people mobilized as "red guards" during the Cultural Revolution later served as social capital when China opened up opportunities for entrepreneurship.

History of the official data in the U.S.

In the initial national income accounts for the U.S. that were released in 1947, government productive outlays on roads, bridges, highways, and ports were not included in the investment category. The conventional view at the time was that government was part of the machinery through which society consumed what was produced by the private sector. Although John Maynard Keynes and his followers insisted in the 1930s and 1940s on the value and importance of government investments, the accounting scheme defined government spending as part of consumption.[10]

Similarly, household spending was also defined as consumption.

While the analysts knew that households could finance both new construction and significant remodeling of existing structures, they chose to simplify the accounts by attributing all residential construction activity to the business sector. Homeowners were treated as renters who were paying rent to themselves. Similarly, household purchases of appliances and automobiles were defined as consumption expenditures even though they were purchased to provide outputs over multiple years. As a consequence of these methodological choices, households were simply not part of the investment economy.

Once this initial framework of analysis was put in place in 1947, very little in the U.S. national income accounts changed for nearly half a century. This was probably the result of the inertial pressures that government statistical agencies face. When such an agency changes its definition of a key category or changes the way that it operationalizes the category, it has the option of drawing a line under a given year and indicating that numbers before and after that line are not strictly comparable because of the change in procedures. However, that strategy undermines the value of the data for users who are relying on comparable historical data. The other option is to apply the redefinition or new operationalization back to all of the earlier years, so that data continuity is maintained. However, that choice involves extensive research work since it is usually the case that relevant data for earlier years will be difficult to find. As a result of this kind of inertia, it was not until the Clinton Administration in the 1990s that the BEA began to revisit its initial definition of investment.

Over close to five decades, the BEA's inertia meant that it ignored several important shifts in mainstream economics. Keynes's recognition that some government spending should count as investment was increasingly accepted by economists. The obvious importance of the Eisenhower Administration's outlays in creating the National Highway System made it difficult to defend the idea that government outlays were unproductive. Moreover, Robert Solow's seminal article showing that increases in economic output could not be explained simply by increased inputs of physical capital and labor focused the attention of the discipline on intangible inputs into production such as technological advances and improvements in employee skills.[11] This was quickly followed by work by Theodore Schultz that argued for the importance of human capital—employee skills—as an input into the production process.[12]

The disjuncture was highlighted by the fact that economists who had worked closely with the BEA published major works that expanded the investment category well beyond what the BEA included.[13] Nevertheless, it was not until a comprehensive revision in 1996 that the BEA began the process of revising its initial concept of investment. The first step was to include governmental expenditures—at local, state, and federal levels—on buildings and equipment as part of the investment category.[14] A second step was taken in 1999 when spending on computer software by both business and government was counted as investment rather than as intermediate goods.[15] This meant going back and reclassifying both purchases of software and the payment to in-house programmers as investment outlays.

A third key revision occurred in 2013 when the BEA introduced a new category of investment: expenditures on intellectual property.[16] This included public and private R&D expenditures, estimated in 2015 at about $500 billion. It also included estimates of what it cost to produce original works of art that were intended to have a long life such as books, movies, and original songs and recordings. This revision followed studies that emphasized the rising importance of these types of intangible investment.[17]

Critique

While the agency has promised further revisions,[18] there is still no indication that it plans to include outlays on education and training in its measure of investment. The likely reason for this resistance is a concern about data continuity. One recent study, for example, conservatively estimated that this type of spending in 2019 would increase domestic investment from $4.5 trillion to $7 trillion.[19] This would add $2.5 trillion to total GDP, increasing it by nearly 12 per cent.

The reluctance might also be linked to a lack of consensus among economists about the proper way to measure human capital investments. One method focuses on tallying up society's outlays on improving the quality of the labor force.[20] The other method seeks to estimate the value of education and training by assuming that the compensation that individuals receive is the flow of services from their accumulated skills.[21] There are two serious problems with this methodology. First, it starts by assuming that the distribution of wage and salary income is a proper reflection of each individual's contribution. So, for example, if compensation at the low end of the labor market is reduced because of exploitation or the market power of employers, this method would significantly overstate the returns on education and training. Second, Abraham and Mallatt effectively show how sensitive the results are to different assumptions.[22] For example, different predictions about whether or not people who have recently dropped out of school will re-enroll have very significant impacts on the resulting estimates.

There is also disagreement as to what outlays count as enhancing the skills and capacities of the labor force. Beyond spending for formal education and training, there is the paid and unpaid labor of raising children from infancy to adulthood. There are also government transfer programs to families with children that help them with the work of childrearing. There are both physical and mental health services that can play a substantial role in expanding people's capabilities.

Also, as noted earlier, the BEA does not include household purchases of consumer durables such as automobiles and appliances in the investment category. This flows logically from their decision to treat homeowners as though they are renting their homes. But these consumer durables obviously produce a flow of services over multiple years for the people who purchase them. Without these appliances, there would be a dramatic escalation in the amount of unpaid labor necessary in the home.

There is, in short, a very substantial gap between what most economists would recognize as investments and what the BEA measures as investment.[23] This gap is a symptom of a paradigm crisis since mainstream economists are not able to align their theoretical conceptions with actual data provided by the government's highly respected statistical agency. Since most econometric studies rely on the official data on investment and GDP, they are using a data set that is problematic and that would likely undermine the validity of their results.

As suggested by Kuhn, when these kinds of anomalies accumulate, it can be a sign that a new paradigm is needed to make sense of what is actually going on.[24] Fortunately, a significant part of that alternative paradigm has already been built by two groups of scholars. The first are those who have elaborated the concept of social reproduction. Social reproduction is usually defined as those activities necessary to produce and sustain the actual human beings who exist in a given society. The second are analysts who have redefined a significant part of public spending as social investment that expands the economy's ability to produce. Combining these two lines of argument point to a new way to conceptualize investment in contemporary economies. Parallel to the classical economists critique of the Physiocrats, this alternative paradigm challenges mainstream economists view of what is productive and what is unproductive.

SOCIAL REPRODUCTION AND SOCIAL INVESTMENT

Feminist theorists immersed in Marxist thought began in the 1970s to argue that both orthodox Marxism and mainstream economists inappropriately privilege the work of production over the work of social reproduction: the process by which human beings are born, nurtured, socialized, and supported over the life course. They argued that this privileging is part of a masculinist worldview that devalues and ignores the types of work that have been largely performed by women. They argued that production is *always* dependent on reproduction; without effective arrangements for reproducing the human population, production would grind to a halt.

Much of the initial work articulating this approach was done by an international feminist group that raised the demand that wages be paid to women for doing housework.[25] Among the principal figures were

Silvia Federici, Mariarosa Dalla Costa, and Selma James. Their point was that capitalism produced two distinct types of exploitation. There was the extraction of surplus value from wage workers and the extraction of work effort from unpaid family members. They argued for political strategies that addressed both types of exploitation. These insights were later elaborated more systematically in a book by Lise Vogel that is often considered the foundation of social reproduction theory.[26]

Over time, the theoretical framework has been further developed to emphasize that housework is part of a larger infrastructure of care work, largely undertaken by women, sometimes unpaid and often poorly compensated as with childcare workers and those paid to care for those with serious health issues.[27] Moreover, it is not just capitalists who benefit from unpaid or poorly compensated care work; beneficiaries include most men and some women. Nevertheless, this care work is central to social reproduction even though its existence has been hidden by liberal theories that assume that autonomous and self-actualizing individuals have little need for care.[28] Recent studies have shown that taking account of unpaid work in the home reshapes economic statistics.[29]

As argued earlier, the habitation concept is an effort to synthesize this focus on social reproduction with other critiques of the existing order. Most importantly, the concept of social reproduction is more capacious than the economist's concept of human capital. The latter focuses narrowly on the acquisition of skills by employees, the former recognizes that present and future workers live in families and communities and their ability to be productive and raise productive offspring depends on an elaborate social infrastructure that includes many hours of unpaid labor in the home by families of different types including single-family households, communes, as well as heterosexual and queer couples. Without this infrastructure, employers would be hard pressed to fill vacancies whether for unskilled or highly skilled employees.

There are, however, tensions within analyses of social reproduction. In some versions, the goal is to undermine the binary that distinguishes "productive labor" from "unproductive labor" since this binary has worked to justify the subordination of women. In other versions, the intention is to demonstrate that work that has historically been devalued as unproductive is, in fact, economically productive. While challenging the binary is useful, the analysis developed here builds on that second strand of social reproduction theory.

Another tension in this body of work centers on questions of causality. Consistent with the Marxist roots of social reproduction theory, some argue that it is inherent in the nature of capitalism that reproduction will always be subordinated to the needs and priorities of production. This means that the crisis of care will only be overcome by transcending capitalism.[30] Others, however, point to significant variations in the public provision of care across developed market societies to suggest that reforms are possible.[31]

The social investment framework

Gøsta Esping-Andersen's *Three Worlds of Welfare Capitalism* (1990) provided a canonical text for the comparative study of social welfare spending by focusing on the degree to which different welfare arrangements reduced people's dependence on labor market earnings. However, in a later book, *Social Foundations of Postindustrial Economies*, Esping-Andersen insisted that postindustrial transformations, including a knowledge economy and much higher rates of female labor force participation, required a re-evaluation of social welfare spending. His argument was explicit in taking on board feminist arguments that mainstream analyses had obscured the importance of women's work, both paid and unpaid.

In the first decades of the twenty-first century, social welfare spending came under increasing pressure in many nations as neoliberals pressed for cutbacks. Scholars, mostly in Europe, responded by building on Esping-Andersen's argument to insist that in the emergent knowledge societies, many of these welfare outlays should be recognized as "social investments" that were contributing to future economic growth.[32] They argued, for example, that government spending for childcare both enhanced future learning for children and increased the availability of mothers for paid labor. Similarly, active labor market policies that provided assistance and retraining for the unemployed should be understood as investments in a skilled labor force. Paid leave for parents that made it easier for two-earner families to raise children were productive because they helped firms retain skilled employees and facilitated effective parenting.

Silja Häusermann *et al.* usefully analyze three dimensions of social investment policies.[33] There is the *creation* of human capital, skills, and capabilities; there is the *mobilization* of these skills and capabilities to be productive in the economy; and there is the *preservation* of these capabilities in the face of disruptions such as unemployment and the dissolution of family ties. Funding for quality childcare would count both for creation and for mobilization since it supports child development while also facilitating the employment of parents of young children. Child allowances can contribute both to the creation of capabilities and for their preservation.

The credibility of the social investment framework is linked to the economic successes of the Nordic nations—Sweden, Norway, Denmark, Finland, and Iceland—along with the Netherlands, all of which rank high in their capacity for innovation. These nations have invested in policies that support women's labor force participation, including publicly funded childcare, along with active labor market policies, and income maintenance programs that leave very few children growing up in poverty.[34] The result has been a labor force with higher levels of adult literacy that has helped firms to compete effectively in the global market.

A new definition

Based on the insights of social reproduction and social investment theories, I propose a new definition of investment. Investment should be understood as *all of the expenditures of money and time required to enhance the capabilities of the population to be productive in the future*. In contrast to the BEA's definition, this one recognizes the importance of education and training and other critical components of social reproduction, including measures to protect the welfare of children. This approach does not privilege reproduction over production; its aspiration is simply to recognize that production and reproduction are equally important and dependent on each other. It follows that all of the elements that are included in the BEA's measure of investment would continue to be included. Outlays on buildings, machinery, expenditures for research and development, and for artistic originals are also important to assure that a high-capability labor force will be productive.

OPERATIONALIZING THE ALTERNATIVE MEASUREMENT SCHEME

Reorganizing categories

The first step in operationalizing this approach is to shift the categories of analysis. In the national income accounts, investment is either made by the private sector or by government since the methodology precludes the idea that households engage in investment activity. The private sector includes the non-profit sector. In this analysis we aggregate household investments with those in the non-profit sector as community investments. These are then contrasted with those by business and government. The non-profit sector's contribution to overall investment is relatively small, but it is appropriate to include it under the community category because its investments are not driven by the search for profits.[35]

In assessing expenditures on buildings, residential, commercial, or governmental, analysts make a distinction between repairs and renovations. Repairs such as a new roof or a paint job do not count as investment since they maintain the building as it is. Renovations, however, count as investments since they add new capacities to the building such as more space or better lighting. In practice, owners often combine repairs and renovations, and taxation systems generally treat investments outlays more favorably. Hence, business tax returns might overstate the dollar value of renovations. Nevertheless, the distinction between repair and renovation makes intuitive sense. It is even more obvious with machinery and vehicles. Repairs are not investments, while replacing an older machine or vehicle is obviously an investment.

With expenditures on human beings, the situation is more complicated. In place of the repair/renovation binary, I am using a three-part category scheme. The equivalent of repairs are maintenance activities required to sustain adult human beings including haircuts, routine medical visits, and various forms of housework including cleaning and meal preparation. As with repairs of physical capital, these are productive activities but they are producing intermediate goods that are used up in the process of production.

The equivalent of renovations are those activities that enhance the skills and capacities of people. This includes education and training expenditures for both children and adults. It also includes childcare outlays and time spent by parents on childrearing. Moreover, when children are in the household (defined here as people under 18), meal preparation and cleaning are necessary for the healthy development of the next generation, so these outlays of time and money are part of enhancing capabilities. The category also includes a portion of healthcare expenditures that restore or enhance capabilities by conquering debilitating illnesses or putting people back together after life-threatening injuries. Various social services that help families cope with major life problems also fall into this category.

The third category is protective maintenance: outlays needed to protect children from circumstances that would undermine their capabilities such as malnutrition or homelessness. Bouts of homelessness can lead to mental health issues that, in turn, undermine the individual's future employability. To be sure, the utility of physical capital can also be undermined by circumstances, such as running a machine continuously without proper lubrication. The difference is that the owners of the machinery usually have both a strong incentive to prevent that from happening and the resources to assure that their employees follow proper maintenance protocols. While children also have strong incentives to protect themselves, they can be powerless to protect against a degradation of their capacities. These expenditures count as investment because they allow children to continue developing their capacities.

This is why programs to maintain the income of households with children such as child allowances, unemployment insurance, food stamps, and social security payments to child survivors should be counted as investment.[36] Without such support, children are at risk to have inadequate nutrition which would impact their cognitive development and ability to learn. Also included here is time that volunteers spend on community organizations that provide services for families in need such as food banks.

It could be argued that protective maintenance outlays for adults should also be counted as investment since their capabilities are at risk of degradation during bouts of unemployment or homelessness. However, they are excluded because I am limiting investment to activities that enhance productive capacity. With children, protective maintenance allows them to continue learning and enhancing their capacities. In many cases with adults, these transfer payments are simply maintaining them as they have been.[37]

Here and elsewhere, I am aiming for defensible consistency even if it ends up somewhat understating the total quantity of investment in the economy. For example, many people who are aged between 19–21 or even older are still developing their capacities, but I am not counting the work of sustaining them as investment activity. I am assuming that they are capable of sustaining themselves, and so only the funds spent on their continuing education or training would be counted as investment.

Moreover, I am also excluding the dollar value of the hours spent either in school or doing homework by both children and adults. This could yield a very large number, but there is no way to estimate the dollar value of those hours since one cannot legitimately hire someone else to do that work. While passing on society's accumulated knowledge to the next generation is an important part of social reproduction, not all of that work needs to be counted in the investment category.

There are also other ambiguous expenditures that I am leaving out of the investment measure. Expenditures by households for various self-improvement efforts such as pursuing hobbies that involve complex skills or teaching oneself a foreign language or computer coding. These could well provide benefits in the future in enhanced capacities, but it seems that the bulk of such outlays are properly seen as consumption expenditures comparable to going to the theater or a music festival.

This is not a definitive list of all the elements that are involved in social reproduction. A case could also be made that some significant portion of the employees at state or local government levels play a critical role in social reproduction, such as public health workers and building inspectors. But generating plausible estimates for these categories is challenging, and the following seven elements are sufficient to reveal the scale of investment with the social reproduction framework. These elements are:

1. Outlays for education and training. This includes the costs paid by government, business, and households for education from kindergarten to advanced degrees. It also includes funds spent by these three entities for formal training of employees.

2. Transfer programs that support families with children. This includes both those programs that protect children from further impoverishment and those that help families raise their children.

3. Healthcare outlays. Some portion of total expenditures on healthcare by government, business, and households represents an investment in improving the capabilities of present and future workers.

4. Childcare outlays. This is an estimate of the dollars spent on providing out-of-home childcare.

5. Non-profit services. This encompasses the outlays of non-profit agencies that provide social services to families, including food banks.

6. Volunteer time. This is an estimate of the dollar value of the labor time spent by people providing services to support their neighbors.

7. Unpaid labor time in families with children. This is an estimate

of the total hours that family members spend on childcare and child maintenance activities, such as meal preparation and cleaning.

In the end, the point of the new framework is that human beings are not robot-like entities that are inserted into workplaces. They are multi-dimensional beings with multiple social ties, family connections, and complex passions and interests. Moreover, their ability to be productive increasingly depends on this multi-dimensionality since many jobs now require some or all of the following capacities: the ability to cooperate effectively with others, problem-solving skills, and a talent for creativity.

A measurement exercise

The revised estimates provided here are necessarily provisional and at times rely on "guesstimates." In some cases, government sources provide reasonable estimates on certain types of outlays that I include as investment. In other cases, such as expenditures for healthcare, only a portion can legitimately be included as investment, but there is no obvious way to calculate what that portion actually is.

While this lack of greater precision is regrettable, use of guesstimates is a standard procedure in the history of economic measurement. Pioneers in economic accounting routinely included such guesstimates in their calculations with the idea that government statistical agencies with more staff and more resources would later on be able to refine those estimates. Those statisticians can add questions to their economic surveys to count outlays that were previously not reported. More recent scholars arguing for revisions in the official accounting scheme continue to utilize guesstimates. It follows that the comparison of the investment data as calculated by the BEA with estimates that operationalize the social reproduction framework is illustrative rather than exact. The intention is to suggest relative orders of magnitude of outlays by different sectors rather than providing some kind of precision.

Table 5.1 presents the current data for gross investment for these three sectors as assessed by the government statisticians. I make three initial adjustments to the BEA figures. First, I shift $813.9 billion of gross residential investment from business to government because in the U.S. most of this is financed by government lending programs that provided $1.3 trillion in real estate loans in 2019.[38] Without this governmental support for the home mortgage market, new investment in residential real estate would be substantially reduced. Second, I move the investments made by the non-profit sector from business to community since they are not driven by the profit motive. Third, I add purchases of consumer durables to the household sector since these are omitted from the BEA numbers. Both the second and third calculation rest on data from the Federal Reserve.

Table 5.1 Comparing the sources of investment, 2019 ($ billions)

	Business investment	**Government investment**	**Community investment**
BEA data	3,826.3	740	0
Residential investment	-798.5	+798.5	
Nonprofit investment[a]	-213.7		+213.7
Consumer durables[b]			+1,413.4
Revised total	2,814.1	1,538.5	1,627.1

[a] This is from line 16, Table F.101 in the Federal Reserve, Flow of Funds Z.1, 9 September 2022.

[b] This is from line 33, Table F.4 in the same source.

Source: BEA, National Income and Product Accounts, Table 5.2.5 Gross and Net Investment by Major Type and Federal Reserve, Flow of Funds. Note that recent revisions to the data have produced minor changes from the numbers reported here.

Note that already with these modifications, the revised total provides a very different understanding of the loci of investment than what is depicted in the top-level BEA number. Business gross investment is exceeded by the combined investments of government and the community sector. This suggests the wisdom of a point that Keynes made back in 1936 in his *General Theory*. He wrote:

> I conceive, therefore, that a somewhat comprehensive socialization of investment will prove the only means of securing an approximation to full employment; though this need not exclude all manner of compromises and of devices by which public authority will co-operate with private initiative. But beyond this no obvious case is made out for a system of State Socialism which would embrace most of the economic life of the community. It is not the ownership of the instruments of production which it is important for the State to assume. If the State is able to determine the aggregate amount of resources devoted to augmenting the instruments and the basic rate of reward to those who own them, it will have accomplished all that is necessary. Moreover, the necessary measures of socialization can be introduced gradually and without a break in the general traditions of society.[39]

Keynes's argument was that the private sector left on its own would not provide a high enough level of investment to achieve anything close to full employment of the existing labor force.[40] This view was based on the British experience in the years after the First World War. Keynes, however, did not believe that government ownership of the means of production was the solution. He believed that through government use of "all manner of compromises and ... devices," the private sector could be induced to invest enough so that in combination with government investment, there would be sufficient total investment to reach full employment.

The devices that Keynes had in mind included use of government lending programs, such as those that undergird the mortgage industry in the U.S. and the Export-Import Bank that helps large firms finance exports. It also included government purchases from industry that come close to $800 billion per year now in the U.S. Then there are tax incentives such as the more rapid depreciation of investments that has significantly reduced the revenue from the corporate income tax as a share of GDP. Finally, there is something that Keynes might not have anticipated, namely the increased investments by the government in science and technology that are discussed in Chapter 3.[41] In a word, governmental measures have been critical to produce the amount of business investment that we see in Table 5.1.[42]

In Table 5.2, we contrast the BEA data with data that is consistent with the new measurement paradigm. Line 1 is the bottom-line number from Table 5.1. (More details as to where additional data come from are provided in the footnotes to Table 5.2.) Line 2 adds expenditures for education and training by business, government, and households. The core item here are the estimates developed by Abraham and Mallatt, but I have added estimates for employee training from other sources.[43]

Table 5.2 Comparing investment through the social reproduction paradigm, 2019 ($ billions)

	Business investment	Government investment	Community investment
Revised total – Table 1	2,814.1	1,538.5	1,627.1
2. Education and training[a]	468.1	1,140.7	962.6
3. Income support[b]		144.4	
4. Healthcare[c]	237.5	569.6	355.7
5. Childcare[d]	16.8	71.8	80.2
6. Nonprofit[e]			246.0
7. Volunteer time[f]			147.0
8. Unpaid work in home[g]			1,855.2
Total	3,536.5	3,465.0	5,273.8
% of total	29%	28%	43%

[a] The basic numbers are drawn from Abraham and Mallatt as provided in their online appendix https://www.aeaweb.org/articles?id=10.1257/jep.36.3.103. These are relatively conservative estimates of actual outlays for education. Their estimate of the value of parental time was subtracted out to avoid double counting for unpaid labor in the

home. The only addition was an estimate of the value of employee training, including the compensation to employees during training periods. This is an estimate drawing on data from *Training Magazine* and Credential Engine. They estimate employer-sponsored training, including direct costs and the compensation for employees while being trained, at $516.1 billion in 2017. We increased the estimate to $550 billion for 2019. Then these were apportioned between business and government by their shares of total employment https://credentialengine.org/wp-content/uploads/2021/02/Education-and-Training-Expenditures-in-the-US.pdf.

[b] Data are from OECD social expenditures database that include outlays by federal and state governments https://www.oecd.org/social/expenditure.htm. For temporary aid to needy families and social security survivor payments for children, 100 per cent of expenditures are included. For unemployment insurance, housing assistance, and food stamps, only 40 per cent is included to count only households with children. With the earned income tax credit, 90 per cent is included because childless families receive only a small share of benefits.

[c] This represents one-third of the healthcare outlays by business, government, and households as reported in U.S. Center for Medical Statistics, National Health Expenditures, Table 5; https://www.cms.gov/Research-Statistics-Data-and-Systems/Statistics-Trends-and-Reports/NationalHealthExpendData/NationalHealthAccountsHistorical.

[d] Public sector childcare outlays are from the OECD social expenditures database. Estimates of business and household childcare expenditures are explained in the text.

[e] Expenditures of non-profits delivering human services are provided for 2016 by Urban Institute, "The Nonprofit Sector in Brief 2019;" https://nccs.urban.org/publication/nonprofit-sector-brief-2019#type. The 2016 number was adjusted upward by 5 per cent to account for growth to 2019. Note that the estimate for non-profit outlays on human services represent less than a third of total outlays for all non-profit entities.

[f] This estimate is based on data from a Current Population Survey and estimates of the value of each hour of volunteer time as provided by Independent Sector; https://americorps.gov/sites/default/files/document/2019%20CPS%20CEV%20findings%20report%20CLEAN_10Dec2021_508.pdf.

[g] The BEA has created a satellite account that estimates the value of household production annually based on time-use studies and a rather conservative rate of hourly compensation; https://www.bea.gov/data/special-topics/household-production. The figure here is 40 per cent of their total since only about 40 per cent of households have a child who is 18 or under.

Line 3 adds income support programs for families with children such as food stamps, TANF, unemployment insurance, social security survivor benefits for children, and outlays to support housing for low-income people as reported in the OECD's social expenditures database. Line 4 adds healthcare expenditures from the National Health Expenditures report prepared by the Center for Medicare and Medicaid Services in the Department of Health and Human Services.[44] It is well known that there is considerable waste in the U.S. healthcare system. Spending per capita is substantially higher than other nations that have better health outcomes. Moreover, it is also estimated that perhaps 10 per cent of all health spending is dedicated to people in the last year of life. Also, some routine medical care should be counted as repair rather than renovation. It follows that only a fraction of total outlays should be counted as investment. To offer a conservative estimate of healthcare investment, the figures on Line 3 represent only one third of total reported healthcare spending in the National Health Expenditures report.

Estimating spending for childcare services is extremely difficult for a number of reasons. There is tremendous variability in arrangements that run from licensed childcare centers to family day care that might or might not be licensed, and a multitude of informal arrangements that might or might not involve payment of money. There are also very substantial differences in cost across different states and the cost of care for infants and toddlers is greater than the cost for children aged three to five. Moreover, there is tremendous variation in the number of hours that children are in such care and that number might change repeatedly over the course of a year.

The problem is compounded by the fact that the government has not sought to systematize data collection on childcare spending. The estimate on Line 4 is a back-of-the-envelope calculation. In 2019, there were 12 million children under five in some form of out-of-home day care.[45] If we assume an average annual price of $14,000, that equals $168 billion.[46] Employers probably cover 10 per cent of this through subsidies and workplace childcare centers, and the OECD indicates that governments at all levels spends $71 billion.[47] The balance of $80.2 billion is paid for by households.[48]

Line 5 provides the outlays of non-profit organizations that provide human services. This category is distinct from health and education non-profits, so it minimizes any possible double counting. Line 6 is an estimate of the value of volunteer time with non-profit groups. Finally, Line 7 provides an estimate of the dollar value of unpaid labor in the home that is calculated by the BEA in a satellite account. These satellite accounts have been created to address inadequacies in the current accounting system without modifying existing estimate of GDP and its components. However, we have included only 40 per cent of the BEA estimate of unpaid household labor since 40 per cent of households include a person age 18 or younger. Moreover, in an earlier study, Jooyeoun Suh and Nancy Folbre estimate the total value of non-market household work in 2010 to be $5.3 trillion, almost 50 per cent higher than the BEA estimate for that year.[49]

When we add up all of those rows in Table 5.2, the results are striking. Gross business investment ends up being small relative to the combined investments of households and government. In Table 5.3, we can clearly see the contrast between these different measurements. The first line shows the BEA data for 2019 with business accounting for 84 per cent of gross investment. The second line provides the BEA data with some adjustments that recognize the role of households and non-profits and acknowledge the importance of government in financing residential investment. The third line shows the measurement under the social reproduction/social investment paradigm. In this estimate, business investment constitutes less than 30 per cent of total investment. Moreover, as we have seen, it has taken the full use of Keynes's compromises and devices to maintain even that level of business investment.

Table 5.3 Comparing three measures, percentage of total investment ($ billions)

	Business investment	**Government investment**	**Community investment**
BEA data (table 1)	3,826.3 (84%)	740 (16%)	
Revised BEA dATA (table 1)	2,814.1 (47%)	1,538.5 (26%)	1,627.1 (27%)
Social reproduction data (table 2)	3,536.5 (29%)	3,465 (28%)	5,273.8 (43%)

If we carried out this same exercise for a European country such as Sweden or Germany where levels of social investment are far higher than in the U.S., the results would be even more dramatic. OECD data, for example, shows that in 2019, Sweden spent close to 3.5 per cent of GDP on public support for families with children.[50] The comparable figure for the U.S. was about 1 per cent. The U.S. would have to increase its spending on children by more than half a trillion dollars to catch up with Sweden.

THE DEPRECIATION ISSUE

All of these calculations focus on gross investment, but the obvious question is whether we would see the same results if we were to focus on net investment. If, for example, investments by the household and by government were to depreciate significantly faster than those of business, then business net investment might account for a significantly higher percentage of total net investment in the economy.

However, this is not the case. While it is not possible here to elaborate a revised scheme for estimating depreciation, there are very strong reasons to believe that the rate of depreciation of public and household investments are substantially slower than those for business whether we are talking about tangible or intangible investments.[51]

Competition and obsolescence

One of the factors that accelerates depreciation for businesses is market competition. A firm making bicycles might be happy to keep using the same factory and equipment for 50 or 60 years, but when a competitor develops a much more efficient production process, the original firm has limited choices. Either it upgrades its equipment and scraps its old machinery, or it simply goes out of business. Either choice ends up with more depreciation.

Neither governments nor households face similar pressures. For example, the statisticians suggest the service life for a military bomber plane is 25 years. However, there are still hundreds of B-52 bombers, first introduced in 1955, that are still in service today. Similarly, the statisticians suggest that the service life of highways and streets are 45 years, but there are many miles of roads that exceed 100 years in use. In fact, the accepted accounting rules for state and local governments indicate that they do not have to depreciate infrastructure at all as long as they have a program for making periodic repairs. We see something similar with households. The service life for furniture for businesses is 14 years. However, in families, substantial pieces of furniture are often handed down from generation to generation. For businesses, the service life for appliances is 9 years, but cookers and white goods routinely are kept in service by families for 20 years or longer.

Another consideration is that a large share of the capital stock of government agencies consists of buildings, some of which have been in place for many decades. While these buildings can decay and become unusable, they are often built on land that has significantly appreciated in value as a consequence of urbanization. It is sometimes possible for both the land and construction costs of a replacement building to be covered by the sale of the appreciated plot of land. In such cases, a calculation of depreciation is meaningless. In contrast, factory buildings, for example, are less likely to be built on land that appreciates dramatically in value.

Depreciation of intangible capital

Figuring out the appropriate service lives of intangible capital investments is a particularly thorny problem. With tangible capital, statisticians can sometimes check their estimates against prices in resale markets. The price of used trucks, airplanes, or older commercial buildings can indicate the realism of estimated service lives. Whether the intangible capital is a computer program, a research and development project, or skills embodied in a particular individual, comparable resale markets either do not exist at all or are far rarer.

Here again, service lives are likely to be considerably longer in the public sector than in the private sector. In the business world, competitive pressures will often force firms to upgrade their computer software, while public agencies are notorious for trying to squeeze yet another year out of a programming language that dates from the 1950s. Moreover, public sector investments in scientific research are tilted more to fundamental research, while private sector investments are concentrated on the development of specific products. The former efforts are likelier to have long-term impacts than the latter. In fact, some research efforts do not depreciate at all. The mapping of the human genome, for example, is bound to produce greater returns with every passing year.

Human skills and capacities

Finally, the largest component of intangible capital are the development of skills and capacities in the population, and the bulk of outlays supporting this come from households and the public sector. Here, also, it is not obvious that these outlays depreciate. Of course, people age, lose capacities, and ultimately die. However, when people learn how to learn, they are able to master new skills through most of their life course. They are not like machines that can do one thing and have to be scrapped when that one thing is no longer needed.

Moreover, over the life course, most of us pass along skills and knowledge to others. This is obvious with parents raising children and with various kinds of teachers. However, in both workplaces and civic organizations, there is a huge amount of informal mentoring and instruction through which skills and capacities are passed down from one generation to the next. Or just think about the total sum of human knowledge in science, social science, and humanities that is preserved in books and journal articles. Some studies suggest that the quantity of scientific publications doubles about every 15 years. Even if one makes some adjustment for declining quality of the average article, this pattern is very different from the limited lifespan of a typical piece of machinery.

In sum, if we were to recalculate Table 5.3 for net investment, the results would be even more dramatic. The business share of total net investment would be even smaller than for gross investment. There is no way around the conclusion that our existing accounting system has provided a false narrative that it is the spending of the business sector that is the key factor in making our economy more productive.

ANALYSIS

The category of investment determines the boundary lines that separate productive expenditures from those that are either unproductive or neutral, as with intermediate goods.

For most of the history of modern economics from Malthus and Ricardo to the first national income accounts in the U.S. in 1947, there was a fairly broad consensus that only the outlays of profit-seeking firms could be counted as investment. It was this perspective that supported familiar arguments for imposing austerity on employees and on government.

Arguments for austerity insist that employees must restrain their demands for higher wages and increased benefits or else businesses will see declining profits that would reduce both the funds available and the incentive for business to make the critical investments required to support current living standards. Similarly, since government outlays are assumed to be unproductive, it follows that taxation represents a deadweight loss that diverts resources that the private sector could use productively. Ronald Reagan described this as government spending being comparable to eating the seed corn that was supposed to be used to produce next year's corn harvest.

However, the numbers in Tables 5.2 and 5.3 suggest a very different story. If households and government are the source of most of the productive investment in the economy, then all of those arguments for austerity disappear. If government has more resources, it can make more productive investments in infrastructure, in R&D, and in strengthening the capacities of the workforce. If households are provided more income, they can also expand their productive investments in their own capacities, those of their children, and those of their neighbors.

Moreover, it follows from Tables 5.2 and 5.3 that investment expenditures by households and government do not "crowd out" private investment, but are more likely to encourage it. For example, government outlays on infrastructure such as highways and airports stimulated massive private sector investments. Similarly, research and development expenditures on computer technology and on medical research have stimulated major investments by high tech firms and biotech firms. More recently, we have seen that government investments in clean energy technologies have stimulated significant amounts of new private sector investment.

A similar point can be made about household investments. We know, for example, that the personal computer itself emerged out of an informal hobbyist subculture, rather than out of major investments by big firms.[52] Moreover, as the market for personal computers took off, there were few resources in society that helped people master the various software packages that facilitated word processing, the creation of spreadsheets, the use of databases, and somewhat later, finding things on the internet. Very few firms had the resources or structures in place to teach people how to make the most effective use of these new tools. The reality is that people taught themselves either individually or in small groups, and their investments of time and energy then facilitated massive levels of business investment to capitalize on the possibilities of these technologies.

CONCLUSION

The point of this measurement exercise is to show that our inherited economic paradigm provides us with a totally false picture of what we need to do to have a more productive economy. In 1900 or even in 1950, it might still have been true that investments by business were the indispensable element for producing economic improvement, but this is no longer the case. In a habitation economy, the outlays by government and households now play this role. The conventional focus on limiting both government spending and wage gains in order to provide the profits and the incentives to drive more business investment is simply wrong. This mistaken focus on austerity for government and households is keeping us from having the habitation that most of us would prefer.

6

Dysfunctional financing

The mismeasurement of investment and the resulting reinforcing of the idea that taxes should be low and that government budgets need to be balanced has played a critical role in undermining the quality of habitation. Ever since the 1970s, subnational levels of government have faced an ongoing fiscal crisis as the demand for services increased faster than the available revenues from taxes. In the U.S., the problem was briefly mitigated by federal revenue sharing, but that policy ended under the presidency of Ronald Reagan. The result has been decaying infrastructure, underfunded services, and an inability to address a growing crisis of housing affordability at the state or local level.

Most significantly, these fiscal pressures have resulted in diminished public spending on education. This is most dramatic in terms of support for public higher education. In many states in the U.S. fees at public colleges and universities were historically quite modest, making it possible for these institutions to be avenues of upward mobility for people from low- and middle-income families. However, for more than 40 years, the trend has been to reduce the amount of public support and rely to an ever-greater extent on tuition payments or student fees. The consequence is that fewer people from low- and middle-income households have been willing to take on the student debt loads required to cover tuition. This, in turn, means that the long historical trend towards higher levels of educational attainment has slowed considerably with other nations catching up and exceeding the U.S.[1]

Moreover, spending on primary and secondary education has also been stagnant with the consequence that compensation for teachers has failed to increase. One study showed that between 1996 and 2021, weekly wages for U.S. school teachers were stable after adjusting for inflation while comparable compensation for other college graduates had increased by 33 per cent.[2] In other words, the ongoing fiscal crisis works precisely to limit the kinds of investment spending that is most critical in a habitation economy.

In the U.S., governments at the state and local level do have the option of borrowing by issuing bonds that are used primarily to finance construction projects: infrastructure, schools, hospitals, and public buildings. The federal government has supported this market by exempting most municipal bonds from federal taxation. This exemption makes the bonds attractive to tax-paying investors even though interest rates are consistently lower than the interest paid on corporate bonds that are taxable.

Nevertheless, in a context of ongoing fiscal crisis, governments are severely constrained in terms of the amount of new borrowing that they can justify. After all, each new bond issue adds interest payments to the expenses that have to be covered by tax revenues. Moreover, in recent years, almost a third of new municipal bond issues are refinancing older debt. The amount of new capital spending being financed is on the order of $200–300 billion per year for all state and local governments across the whole country. This is a drop in the bucket since the infrastructure deficit identified by the American Civil Engineers is $2.6 trillion over the next ten years, and their calculation does not include affordable housing.[3]

Finally, this mode of financing intensifies the divide between states and localities that are growing in population and those that are declining. Rising population makes it easy to project future growth in tax revenues that justify new borrowing while declining population does the opposite. The consequence is that places suffering population loss are less able to borrow to finance investments that could lead to economic renewal. The logic of the municipal bond market makes it virtually impossible to borrow one's way to renewed prosperity.

SPECULATIVE EXCESSES

The failure of the tax and financial systems to provide sufficient funding for infrastructure and affordable housing is just the tip of the iceberg of a dysfunctional financial regime. The irony of this financial regime is that there is an ongoing capital glut; there are vast amounts of funds in search of profitable investment opportunities. And, at the same time, most of the productive forms of investment are systematically being deprived of the capital that is needed. The consequence is a huge amount of wasteful and potentially destructive speculative activity while productive investments are ignored and starved of capital.

The core problem is that the Anglo-American financial system was built around the needs of the corporations of the industrial era. In the first half of the twentieth century, issuance of stocks and bonds by private firms financed the creation of giant corporate empires. However, once those corporate empires were created, many of the major firms became self-financing. They were able to use profits and generous depreciation allowances to finance new investment without the need to raise new money from the sale of stocks and bonds. However, successful self-financing meant that previously issued shares would continually rise in value as profits per share continued to increase. The result was that a rising stock market consistently attracted ever more investment money.

This trend was intensified by the financialization of retirement that was driven by two convergent trends. First, business firms were eager to abandon defined benefit pension plans that offered retirees a fixed amount of funds for each year of service. These plans forced firms to put funds aside to cover these future expenses. As of 1980, there were 30 million private sector employees covered by such plans, but this number had fallen to slightly more than 10 million in 2019. Firms switched instead to defined contribution plans that put a set amount per employee in an account that was invested in stocks and bonds. In 1980, there were fewer than 20 million employees in such plans, but this number increased to 85 million by 2019.[4] Most of these corporate plans were administered by a small handful of firms including Fidelity,

Vanguard, and BlackRock that ultimately became the largest holders of corporate equities.[5]

At the same time, free market activists who opposed social security benefits because it represented a huge burden on the federal budget recognized that the only way to dismantle the system was by creating a growing pool of middle-class people who would not be dependent on social security benefits because they had other forms of retirement savings. They agitated for the creation of various tax-deferred savings plans such as individual retirement accounts (IRAs) to help create a much larger pot of retirement saving for people in the top half of the income distribution.[6] While the strategy created vast new pools of savings that were invested in stocks and bonds, there was still strong public opposition to the privatizing of social security when it was pushed by President George W. Bush in 2005.

The consequence of these parallel developments was that every year, through defined contribution plans and IRAs, hundreds of billions of new dollars flowed into the stock market even in years of recession. This created a durable upward bias to stock prices even as most firms had become self-financing. For decades now, the stock market as a whole actually returns money to households rather than drawing funds from households. Individual firms may raise new money by issuing stocks, but this is offset by the flows from established firms through share buybacks.

Up until 1982, firms were prohibited from purchasing their own shares; it was seen as a form of market manipulation. However, the Reagan Administration changed the rules and allowed these transactions.[7] This occurred at a time when executive compensation had shifted from salary to stock options and stock grants and when corporations were being pressured to maximize shareholder value. The idea was that if top executives owned or had the option to purchase large numbers of shares, they would more closely align their interests as managers with the interests of shareholders.

Not surprisingly, firms have responded by increased reliance on share buybacks rather than dividends as a way to return profits to shareholders. The reason is obvious; buybacks, by reducing the number of shares available on the open market, are a more reliable mechanism than dividends for boosting the firm's share price. And since executive compensation has been tied to the share price, this is a more effective way for those same executives to increase their compensation. Boosting dividends might also support the firm's stock price, but it is difficult to increase dividends if profits are not increasing. However, buybacks can be undertaken even when earnings are disappointing. Moreover, it is not uncommon for firms to finance buybacks by issuing bonds.

By the 2020s, share buybacks had soared to close to $1 trillion per year. These are funds that are being returned to both individual shareholders and institutional shareholders. These flows over the last 40 years have set in motion a frantic search for new asset classes that could provide comparable returns to the stock market. This helps to explain a series of asset price bubbles as speculative funds flowed into one or another of these asset classes including "junk bonds" in the 1980s, internet startup firms in the 1990s (the dot-com bubble), and collateralized mortgage obligation (CMO) bonds in the 2000s. It was massive flows to purchase high-yielding CMOs based on subprime mortgage lending that led to the global financial crisis in 2008–09.[8]

More recently, cryptocurrencies have been the exciting new asset class that has drawn huge amounts of investment. At the peak in 2021, the market capitalization of crypto firms globally had reached nearly $3 trillion, and it was still over $1 trillion by the middle of 2023.[9] In contrast to other fashionable asset classes, with crypto there is no persuasive claim that the funds flowing into the asset will produce some future flow of resources. It seems rather to be an argument that the value of Bitcoin or Ethereum will continue to rise because demand will grow faster than supply, allowing current investors to benefit from the anticipated price rise.

The other new asset class that has continued to grow in size while other asset classes go through periods of boom and bust has been the market for derivative instruments that allow investors to take positions on the future of currency exchange rates, interest rates in different markets, and the likelihood that bond issuers might default. The total value of over-the-counter derivative contracts reached $630 trillion by 2022. Admittedly, this figure counts both sides of a contract and most of these contracts are purchased on margin, so investors have put up only a fraction of this amount. Nevertheless, it remains the case that many trillions of dollars are being invested in these instruments.

The justification for markets in derivatives is that they help to smooth out the workings of financial markets by giving people and institutions the opportunity to hedge against adverse market developments. The claim is by mitigating risk, the availability of derivatives encourages higher levels of productive investment. However, there have been clear instances where derivative markets have intensified speculation and contributed to financial instability. For example, both credit default swaps and foreign exchange derivatives make it much easier to speculate against a particular nation's currency. We have seen a number of instances where a government is forced to abandon a fixed exchange rate, and the speculative activity overshoots producing an immediate devaluation that is much larger than what might be needed to restore some balance in the nation's foreign transactions.

But the ultimate issue is that the world would be much better off if the trillions invested in derivatives contracts had instead been spent on addressing the challenge of climate change, both reducing the use of fossil fuels and making people's habitation more resilient in the face of more frequent extreme weather events. However, our financial institutions produce a systematically perverse outcome. Although there is an ample annual flow of retirement savings in the U.S., most of it is directed into the purchase of corporate stocks and bonds. However, since the corporations are self-financing, the money goes back out in the form of buybacks to the wealthy and financial institutions, and these, in turn, in a constant search for higher yields, fund investments that are often speculative, unproductive, and disruptive.

SYSTEMATIC UNDERFUNDING

This speculative logic plays out at the same time that five critical parts of the habitation economy are systematically deprived of financing at reasonable interest rates.

Affordable housing

Even with substantial government involvement in the housing sector, especially in helping to provide mortgage finance at reasonable interest rates, the supply of affordable housing has continued to shrink. On the one hand, the government stopped adding to the public housing stock back in the Nixon Administration. The government does offer a tax credit to incentivize the development of low-income housing, but the scale of the program remains much too small.

The core problem is that given effective interest rates and the multiple risks of construction projects, developers of multi-family housing have every incentive to focus their efforts on the high end of the real estate market. It is sometimes claimed that as more affluent households trade up to newer housing, older buildings will trickle down to lower-income households. But we actually see the opposite dynamic at work in many urban areas where gentrification results in more affluent households bidding up the cost of housing and real estate taxes, so that less affluent households are displaced and end up swelling the ranks of those forced to spend more than half their earnings on housing.

Infrastructure

We have already seen that state and local governments have lacked the resources to make needed investments in infrastructure. And since most infrastructure takes the form of public goods, private businesses are unlikely to make such investments without either government purchases or substantial subsidies. So even when there is ample evidence of substantial economic benefits from a particular infrastructure project, it is unlikely to happen unless funding is provided by the federal or state government.

Higher levels of labor force skills

While the U.S. funds a number of small-scale public efforts to provide employees with higher levels of vocational skills, both the U.S. and the U.K. lack the kind of active labor market policies pursued by various European governments.[10] The consequence is that employees who want to upgrade their skills usually have to finance such efforts by themselves, and they have to contend with a largely unregulated for-profit training industry that often fails to deliver the job opportunities it promises. Some U.S. community colleges have launched vocational programs linked to local labor market needs, but these efforts have not yet been scaled up through significant federal funding.

The irony is that the U.S. has made massive use of public lending to help finance the rising cost of higher education with total student debt now at $1.78 trillion. However, this is deeply irrational as public policy. Many people in their twenties, thirties, forties, and even later, are burdened with substantial debt repayments. Moreover, the risks of long-term indebtedness deter young people from the bottom half of the income distribution from pursuing higher education. It would have been far more rational as public policy for the federal government to provide state governments with the funds needed to keep tuition fees at public colleges and universities at levels that would continue accessibility for people from low-income families.

Small enterprises: non-profit and for-profit

Small enterprises, including high tech startup firms, struggle continuously with access to capital at reasonable interest rates. As the banking sector has consolidated, fewer banks are involved in lending to small businesses. Their characteristic response is to urge entrepreneurs to put expenses on the credit card with interest rates often exceeding 20 per cent. The major exceptions are real estate developers who are able to provide collateral in the form of land or buildings that provide financial institutions with some insurance against a failure to repay the loan.

The government created the Small Business Administration to deal with this issue by providing loan guarantees for banks. However, total SBA lending authority has typically been limited to around $44 billion per year, a small amount given that there are possibly 33 million small businesses. In 2023, those businesses lucky enough to qualify end up paying somewhere between 8–13 per cent in interest. This means that SBA loans are not an option for many small businesses and non-profits that would be able to handle a loan at 4 or 5 per cent.

Think of a non-profit or an entrepreneur who needed a loan of $100,000 to launch a childcare center. The difference between paying $4,000 each year in interest versus $13,000 might well make it impossible to create a business plan that would generate enough future surplus to pay down the initial loan. Similar calculations might deter a variety of arts organizations that wanted to open a gallery or form a local theater company. In each of these cases, there might be thousands of separate initiatives that were not pursued because of this daunting interest rate mathematics. The consequence is impoverished habitation as services that could have been available are not since the needed funds went instead to acquire cryptocurrencies.

The absence of lending at reasonable rates also blocks the opportunity for upward mobility through small-scale entrepreneurial activities. As noted earlier, some of these market niches have already been taken over by larger firms. But some of those that remain, such as launching a food truck or renovating run-down residences, requires a significant amount of start-up capital, so the path is often closed to those who cannot borrow the funds from friends and relatives.

The absence of affordable financing is a particularly acute problem for technology startups. Every year, thousands of such firms are started by one or a few technologists with an idea for a new product or service. The federal government has established the Small Business Innovation Research program (SBIR) that directly funds close to 7,000 of such firms each year. These are the survivors of a rigorous review process that assesses 40,000–50,000 applications.

However, the firms that are successful in gaining both a Phase I and a Phase II grant usually receive enough money to operate for three years. However, it often takes five to ten years for these firms to get to a commercial product that will bring in revenue. So even with SBIR success, many of these firms have to find a way to survive from the time when SBIR funding ends and the arrival of commercial revenue—the valley of death.[11]

The small percentage of such firms that can project rapidly growing future revenues are often able to receive funding from angel investors or from venture capitalists since they can make substantial profits when the firm either makes an initial public offering of its stock or is acquired by an existing firm. However, most of these firms are looking at a niche market that might grow at 20 or 30 per cent a year, but they have no prospect of being the next Facebook or Google. For many, the only survival option is to be acquired by a bigger company. However, as we noted earlier, this is risky since the acquiring firm might eventually decide against bringing the new product to market.

Policymakers are acutely aware of the difficulties that these small firms face. Many state governments have established programs that provide matching funds to successful SBIR firms with the idea that such resources could help firms survive the valley of death. In 2021, the Biden Administration revived an Obama-era program, the State Small Business Credit Initiative (SSBCI) with an additional $10 billion of funds. These funds were divided across state governments and were targeted to help small businesses and non-profits through credit programs, loan guarantees, or venture capital funding. However, this was a one-shot initiative that was included in the Covid recovery bill, and much of the funding had already been distributed by June of 2023.[12]

Clean energy and conservation

In face of the climate crisis, it is obvious that not enough money is being spent on reducing the burning of fossil fuels both through the development and deployment of clean energy and pursuing initiatives to use energy much more efficiently. It is well known that small measures such as improving the insulation of buildings and shifting to LED lighting can pay for themselves in three or four years. Nevertheless, banks and other financial institutions have shown little interest in offering loans to finance such expenditures for households or businesses. The same thing is true in terms of funding for installing solar panels on roofs or for shifting from gas or oil burning furnaces to heat pumps. The shortsightedness of this financing policy is now increasingly obvious as nations around the world face the enormous costs associated with extreme weather events and ever-rising temperatures.

A number of green financing initiatives at the state level in the U.S. have used subsidies and loan guarantees to demonstrate that large-scale financing of clean energy and conservation for both residences and businesses is both feasible and financially sound. These initiatives paved the way for the Biden Administration's Inflation Reduction Act, passed in 2022, that makes massive use of tax credits, loan guarantees, and subsidies to encourage green expenditures. Some estimates suggest that the legislation could produce a trillion dollars in green investments over a ten-year period. It remains uncertain whether this initiative will be sustained over time, but the effort does demonstrate what the priorities would be of a rational and environmentally sound financial system.

ALTERNATIVE FINANCING

In the previous chapter, I showed that government is already funding almost as large a percentage of total investment as the private sector. The IRA suggest an alternative pathway in which public policies play a much larger role in directing finance into productive channels. However, there are two myths or illusions that continue to block that pathway.

The first myth is that capital available for investment is scarce, so we have no choice but to assure those with substantial savings a high level of return. This is, of course, the foundation of all "trickle down" economics. The idea is that we must maintain a high rate of profitability, even after taxation, or the vital investments that society needs will not take place. Since we have already seen that communities and government account for the bulk of productive investment, this claim is obviously false. But it is even worse than that since corporations in the aggregate are self-financing, so that some of the huge savings of the rich and the accumulated retirement savings of everyone else end up pursuing asset price bubbles or cryptocurrencies.

The second myth is the idea that financial institutions, such as banks, are intermediaries who draw savings from depositors and then loan those funds to borrowers who make investments. This idea complements the belief in capital scarcity since it requires that public policy be deferential to bankers or they will cease intermediating and the economy will grind to a halt. The reality, however, is that banks and other financial institutions are licensed by the government to create credit that is then validated by government agencies including the Federal Reserve and the Department of the Treasury.

In the terminology developed by Robert Hockett, the government has the franchise to create money.[13] It extends that power to banks and other financial institutions in much the same way that McDonald's extends the power to make its burgers and fries to its franchisees. In the corporate world, firms like McDonald's keep a close regulatory eye on their franchisees to make sure that they are upholding the franchiser's often exacting standards. The government also needs to keep a close regulatory eye on its franchisees, but the myth of financial intermediation allows banks to push back against those regulations.

The contradiction is that banks make greater profits when they take on more risk.[14] They can charge more interest, for example, by lending to less creditworthy borrowers. They can also earn higher returns the more money they lend. Since they are managed to maximize profit, they always have an incentive to increase the riskiness of their holdings. The only constraints are the regulations enforced by the franchiser. However, when the regulators are encouraged to go easy, or pursue what the British call "light touch" regulations, the risks will escalate. When the riskiness grows too great, some banks will be in danger of collapse. However, the franchiser, in the end, will inevitably bail out the banks since the consequences of strings of bank failures are potentially catastrophic.

This is the ridiculous cycle in which we have been stuck for decades. Giant banks took on too much risk by lending to the developing world in the late 1970s and early 1980s. The government bailed them out. Savings and loan associations took on too much risk in the 1980s buying junk bonds. The government bailed them out. In the 1990s, we had the internet stock bubble, but since banks were only marginally involved, there was no need for a bailout. In the 2000s, banks and other financial institutions took on too much risk by acquiring bonds backed by dubious real estate loans. The government bailed them out in 2008 and 2009. Again in 2023, a handful of regional banks put too much money into bonds that declined in value when interest rates rose. The government bailed them out once again. The Dodd–Frank bill passed in 2010 was supposed to put an end to banks being "too big to fail," but since then the biggest banks have gotten even bigger, making bailouts even more necessary.

Once we reject the myths of capital scarcity and banks as financial intermediaries, a more rational approach comes into view. Instead of concentrating the money-creation franchise on for-profit entities, the government could greatly expand the number and size of franchisees who are organized as non-profit entities. Regulation will still be necessary, but stripped of the imperative to maximize profits, these institutions could focus their credit-creating capacity on achieving broader social goals such as reducing poverty and reducing greenhouse gases.

There is ample evidence that such non-profit financial initiatives are feasible and sustainable.[15] For more than a century, the State Bank of North Dakota has played a critical role in underpinning that state's economy and in supporting family farmers. Credit unions, community banks, and community development financial institutions (CDFI) have successfully weathered economic downturns without the need for the periodic bailouts that have become routine for commercial banks. The Obama Administration made use of the Department of Energy's Loan Guarantee Program to support $28 billion in investments designed to drive forward innovation in clean energy technologies. While the program suffered some defaults, the lifetime cost of the lending was estimated in 2014 to be only $2.2 billion.[16] Given these results, the Biden Administration dramatically increased the lending capacity of this program as part of the Inflation Reduction Act.

It is important, however, that any effort to move from the current predominantly for-profit financial system to a predominantly not-for-profit system should emphasize decentralization, competition, and democratic input. One of the big problems with the existing financial system is the concentration of power in a handful of giant firms: the biggest commercial banks and the biggest fund managers. This, in turn, encourages monocropping or pressure on all large borrowers to conform to the guidelines and expectations of the people who run these firms. We have seen this particularly with the pressure on corporate managers to maximize shareholder value despite the fact that boosting the short-term share value might hurt the firm over the longer term.

If a non-profit financial system were highly concentrated as in some proposals for creating a centralized national investment authority, it would reproduce this same dynamic. Potential borrowers would likely have nowhere else to turn, so they would be forced to conform to whatever were the biases of that centralized organization. Moreover, a firm with what most people saw as a heterodox technology idea would have no opportunity of funding to explore the feasibility of its idea. Moreover, even if such an agency were initially staffed with only altruistic and public-spirited employees, the chances are very high that eventually those at the top of such an organization would come to believe that they were entitled to wealth and status commensurate with their power.

While there is obviously a need for some centralized coordination and information pooling, the goal should be to have multiple non-profit financing agencies operating in an environment that encourages both competition and cooperation. Competition will encourage multiple firms to gain expertise in lending for certain purposes such as particular types of infrastructure or a particular type of technology. Cooperation is also necessary since in some cases, several of these entities would need to collaborate to finance certain large-scale projects. There would also need to be a wide variety of financing instruments of different durations, including some that would give the lender a share of the borrower's future earnings. There would also need to be loan guarantees for higher risk lending that fulfilled a public purpose.

Finally, this new financial system would require new mechanisms of democratic accountability to assure that the flows of investment capital are consistent with the preferences of voters. However, there is no singular institutional solution that will work across a multiplicity of different financial entities. With smaller-scale organizations such as credit unions and CDFIs, their organizational leadership could be held accountable by votes of the membership or a community board. Public banks, created by cities and states, could be required to have a board that is representative of the local population. Larger public infrastructure banks might be required to give veto power over lending to advisory boards that were broadly representative. Alternatively, temporary deliberative bodies such as citizen assemblies could be used to approve or disapprove of major projects.

Moreover, one way to assure greater public control over habitation is to require that larger local infrastructure projects be approved through referenda. So even before the locality sought financing for a particular project, local voters would have given their approval. Here again, citizen assemblies could be used to finetune competing priorities, so that the plan presented to voters would be one that reflected considerable citizen input.

SUPPORTING COOPERATIVE NETWORK PRODUCTION

I showed earlier that the existing stock market-centered system of finance is largely inhospitable to cooperative network production since it is focused on strengthening hierarchical firms. Many startup firms have no choice but to sell themselves to one of the established corporations with the considerable risk that their particular technology will never reach the market. There is an acute need for an alternative system of financing that would support small and medium-sized enterprises that are focused on a particular market niche and are not interested in the kind of spectacular growth that is an obsessive concern of most venture capitalists.

Moreover, both in the United States and abroad, there have been many examples of successful small and medium-sized firms that have assembled high levels of specialized expertise that facilitates ongoing innovation and high levels of product quality. Historically, the U.S. machine tool industry was dominated by such firms. Germany's ongoing success in manufacturing is often attributed to the Mittelstand: medium-sized, often family-owned, firms that have developed significant capacities for innovation and high-quality production. Not surprisingly, these firms have been able to draw on financing from Germany's considerable network of non-profit banks, both cooperative banks and the Landesbanken that were historically owned by provincial governments.

In the innovation space, there are concrete cases that demonstrate that important advances can be made without the technologists expecting to become millionaires or billionaires. There are several employee-owned firms such as PSI (Physical Sciences Inc.) that have been repeatedly successful in winning SBIR grants to develop new technologies. Since these firms want to retain their eligibility for that program, they deliberately keep their number of employees below 500. When a new technology is ready for the market, they spin off a new startup to develop that product. This is an institutional solution that allows scientists and engineers to have considerable control over the conditions of their work while working on practical technological puzzles. It also demonstrates that cooperative network production can flourish outside of the standard corporate form. Hierarchies of wealth and power are not a precondition of innovation.

However, different kinds of financial institutions are necessary to sustain an economic system of cooperative network production built around small and medium-sized firms. Stock-market financing is to be avoided precisely because it rewards growth more than stability. Non-profit banks that combine business lending with standard retail banking would be the best solution. They would provide these firms with ongoing banking services and help them raise capital for major projects that cannot be financed out of earnings. The largest loans would require the participation of multiple non-profit banks.

Two additional innovations would be needed to make this work. First, the loans for capital projects would grant the lenders both a fixed interest rate and a small share of future profits.[17] This profit share is necessary to offset the risk of those loans that default because a small or medium-sized business is unable to cover its debts. Moreover, each of these banks would limit its riskier loans to a level that could be covered by reserves.

Second, there would also need to be a system of loan guarantees to share the considerable risks involved in lending to startup firms that have a considerably higher chance of going out of business. A number of European countries have created systems of loan guarantees for start-ups that divide the risk between the lending agency and a number of other entities. Such a system obviously requires screening mechanisms that eliminate firms with little prospect of success. However, the survival of the guarantee schemes indicates that the risks can be effectively managed.

This kind of financing system would be ideal for sustaining an innovative system of cooperative network production built around small and medium-sized businesses. Such a system could generate ongoing technological advances without the ongoing increases in income and wealth inequality that characterize our current production system.

CONCLUSION

There are multiple ways in which the existing financial system stands in the way of people getting the kind of habitation that they want and need. Not only does the current system starve state and local governments of the resources needed to address public needs, but it has also provided ongoing funding for the fossil fuels that endanger the planet while neglecting to finance clean energy and energy conservation. Furthermore, the existing financial system has created multiple asset price bubbles that have resulted in financial crises and costly public bailouts of "too big to fail" private financial institutions.

However, another type of financial system that would support improved habitation and cooperative network production is entirely feasible. Precisely because credit creation by banks and other financial entities is dependent upon the central government, it is possible for the government to incrementally shift that credit-creating franchise to non-profit financial intermediaries that would redirect credit in productive and environmentally sustainable directions.

7

Democratizing habitation

This book has sought to illuminate the centuries-old conflict between habitation and improvement. Improvements in the form of technological advances have frequently undermined the habitation of many people. I have tried to show, however, that we have the possibility of channeling improvements in directions that would actually improve the habitation for all people. But this potential is not being realized within the existing political-economic constraints that drastically limit the ability of people to shape their own communities. The urgent task is to democratize the creation of habitation and this requires reforms that allow people to exercise greater control over the soft and hard infrastructures of the communities in which they live.

The intensification of the climate crisis has made the task of democratizing habitation ever more urgent. Climate scientists have been warning for decades of the dangers of continuing to pump more and more greenhouse gases into the earth's atmosphere, but it has only been in the decade of the 2020s that the negative consequences have become undeniably obvious. Extreme heat, uncontrollable wild fires that darken the sky for thousands of miles, devastating droughts, ever more powerful hurricanes, typhoons and tornadoes, floods, and other extreme weather events have become increasingly common. Everyone's habitation and even their survival are now threatened by the reality of climate change.

Responding to this threat requires two connected initiatives that would be accelerated by democratizing habitation. The first is to speed up the shift to energy conservation and the use of renewables so that societies could more quickly lower the production of greenhouse gases. Whatever initiatives have been put into place by central governments are bound to move more quickly if and when people at the local level are actively engaged in reducing their community's dependence on fossil fuels. At the same time, those local initiatives would place more pressure on central governments to move more boldly and spend more money on the effort.

The second initiative is increasing the resilience of local communities, so that people are better protected against extreme heat, flooding or other climate-related disasters. This can involve everything from major infrastructure projects to redirect water flows to the creation of cooling centers to organizing self-help initiatives at the neighborhood level. Moreover, as more people become involved in efforts to protect themselves and their neighbors from climate-related disasters, this would increase pressure on both local and national officials to fund major resilience projects and to accelerate the shift away from fossil fuels.

The cost–benefit analysis to justify very substantial outlays to address climate change and resilience is straight forward. The National Centers for Environmental Information maintains a database on the climate-related disasters that generate costs of $1 billion or more with adjustments for inflation.[1] In the 2000s, there was an average of 6.7 of these events each year. In the past five years, the average has increased to 18 per year, and in 2023, there were 28 events. In 2022, the cumulative cost of these events was $177 billion, but expenditures can be expected to go much higher. In 2017, when there were three major hurricanes that impacted urban areas, the total cost for that year rose to $383.7 billion in inflation-adjusted dollars.

Moreover, these calculations focus primarily on property damage and the costs of rebuilding structures. There is no effort to estimate the value of the human lives lost, the mental health burden following on such disasters, and the impact on families of losing loved ones. In fact, estimating heat-related deaths is difficult since death certificates often attribute death to underlying conditions such as heart disease rather than high temperatures. But one study estimated that Europe's extremely hot summer temperatures in 2022 resulted in 62,000 deaths that would not have happened otherwise.[2] It is not difficult to imagine the number of such deaths from extreme heat in the U.S. exceeding 100,000 a year in the absence of effective public policies.

Moreover, it is important to emphasize that the populations most at risk from climate-related disasters are the elderly, the poor, immigrants, and those who have suffered most from racism—African Americans, Latinos, and Native Americans. These are the people most likely to live without air conditioning and in substandard housing and who have jobs that requires them to work outdoors.

THE THEORY

The project of democratizing habitation builds on a body of work that emphasizes the limitations and dangers of representative democracy and argues for more participatory and more deliberative forms of democratic governance.[3] The argument is that representative democracy tends to create a growing divide between a political class, made up of elected officials from the major political parties, and ordinary voters who feel largely powerless to influence decisions made by both legislatures and executives in central governments where both political power and critical economic decisions have been concentrated. The explanation for this division between the political class and everyone else is what was laid out by Robert Michels more than a century ago.[4] Elected officials have access to information and organizational resources that ordinary voters lack, and they are able to use both to perpetuate their hold on power. While the relative electoral fortunes of particular political parties will fluctuate over time, it is still members of the same political class who move in and out of the most powerful positions.

Moreover, this creates a downward spiral. Many voters whose political participation consists of showing up at a polling place every two to four years have little opportunity to understand how the political process works or how to effectively make their own voices heard. In theory, local politics should operate as a training ground where the gap between the political class and ordinary voters is reduced. However, as we have seen earlier, local politics is characterized by zero-sum conflicts over extremely limited resources and the entrenched influence of powerful local interests such as real estate developers and large corporations. This generates cynicism and disengagement from local politics.

It is this downward spiral of disillusionment with representative democracy that creates openings for demagogues who promise to "drain the swamp" and end the corrupt practices of the existing political class. Such anti-political arguments resonate with some voters who are alienated from politics and feel that the existing system is rigged against them. Warning such voters that their preferred candidate will undermine democratic norms and institutions can be an exercise in futility since they have already lost faith in the idea of democracy.

It follows from this critique that an effective system of representative democracy requires a significant expansion of citizen participation in decision making. This participation would increase citizen understanding of the political process and would teach the skills required for citizens to effectively articulate and advocate for their own interests. With widespread mechanisms for participation, an intermediate group would be formed between ordinary voters and the political class. These grassroots leaders would have similar skills and resources to those people in the political class, and they could help citizens assure that elected representatives are held accountable to their constituents. Moreover, those grassroots leaders would be available to replace elected representatives who proved to be unresponsive.

There are many potential mechanisms to drive this increase in political participation. One idea builds on the use of juries in the legal system where citizens are asked to make decisions on guilt or innocence or on whether individuals should be charged with certain crimes. In deliberative assemblies, groups of ordinary citizens are provided testimony from multiple experts and then asked to decide on key issues of public policy such as the location and nature of investments in infrastructure or the drawing of legislative districts. Deliberative assemblies can be combined with greater use of referenda. The assembly might formulate rival proposals, and then voters would have the opportunity to choose among competing plans for using local resources.

In participatory budgeting, citizens have the opportunity to assemble and choose among different options for local budget priorities.[5] Another option is to expand the role of elected citizen boards for determining local policies in particular domains. For example, some cities responded to episodes of racist policing by establishing elected civilian review boards that could discipline police officers found to have acted wrongly. In the same way that local school boards are filled through elections, one might have local health boards, infrastructure boards, and so forth.

However, virtually all of these schemes for expanding citizen participation have been frustrated by the reality of limited budget resources. Localities routinely do not have sufficient revenue to fund their existing commitments. The consequence is that when citizens participate, they end up in zero-sum conflicts where one neighborhood might win at the expense of other neighborhoods. Such zero-sum conflicts tend to worsen cynicism about politics and reinforce alienation from the political system.

The strategy proposed here is to wed various mechanisms for increasing citizen participation with significant increases in the resources available to localities. The increased resources would come both through shifting tax revenues from the central government down to localities and by improving access of localities to borrowing at favorable interest rates. The increased resources would significantly expand the efficacy of participation and create a virtuous cycle of greater citizen involvement in the project of self-governance.

THE NATURE OF THE STRATEGY

The project of democratizing citizen control over habitation would initially emphasize questions of climate change and climate justice, but it is a strategy that could also address many of society's most pressing problems including racial injustice, extreme economic inequality, the subordination of women and sexual minorities, and alienated labor. As a political project, it would be classified as radical reformism because it envisions an incremental process of change in which immediate reforms create the conditions for succeeding cycles of reform. It sees democratization as an open-ended process that gives people greater voice and influence on governments at all levels. As more people learn the skills of governing themselves, the current gap in power and understanding between people and their elected representatives would narrow.

The project would play out at multiple levels. While much of the initial work would focus on organizing people within communities—big cities, small cities, small towns, and rural counties—there would be a parallel focus on influencing state governments and the central government since it is those levels that control access to funding. Moreover, there would also be a need to organize and mobilize at the level of supranational regional groupings such as the European Union, the U.S.–Mexico–Canada Agreement in North America, and Mercosur in South America. There also need to be incremental reforms of the rules governing the global economy that are enforced by institutions such as the World Bank, the International Monetary Fund, the Bank for International Settlements, and the World Trade Organization.

The strategy is built on the idea that political and economic reforms at the local level are constrained by higher levels of governance. Movements at the local level would form coalitions to push for changes at the level of state or provincial governments. Those coalitions would, in turn, build alliances to gain changes at the central government level that could facilitate major reforms. National movements would then need to coalesce together to reshape policies of supranational governance at both the level of supranational regions and at the level of global institutions. At each of these levels, one focus of the struggle would be to gain control of more resources that could be funneled down to communities both large and small. The work of creating more space and more resources at the local level where habitation is created and recreated would happen through multiple cycles of contestation and reform.

However, any strategy for political change must confront the issue of feasibility, and feasibility has both a political and an economic dimension. Political feasibility depends on showing that this particular strategy has a better chance of succeeding than other potential strategies. Many radical reform projects of the past 50–60 years have ended in defeat or disaster. However, Thomas Piketty's work has shown that between 1914 and 1970, reformist movements were successful in many developed market societies in achieving significant reductions in the inequality of income and wealth.[6] Nevertheless, for the past half-century, the very rich have regained the political initiative and have been successful in places such as the United States and the United Kingdom in restoring income and wealth inequality to levels not seen since the nineteenth century. Moreover, global oligarchs have invested heavily in sophisticated organizational networks and media tools that are intended to preserve their political power.

Nevertheless, Piketty's account suggests that since oligarchic power was successfully challenged in an earlier period, another challenge could possibly succeed against what are formidable obstacles. Given those obstacles, it is not a question of proving that the democratizing habitation strategy has a high probability of success. The task is rather to show that it has significant advantages over other strategies. How might a politics based on democratizing habitation build a powerful majoritarian coalition in multiple places? How might this strategy overcome the logic of political polarization where strong left-wing political movements have been matched or more than matched by the growing electoral success of far-right political parties or political factions.

The economic dimension of feasibility centers on showing that a political strategy can produce a significant and durable improvement in most people's sense of well-being. This has proven a formidable hurdle for attempts by elected leaders to carry out radical reforms in places such as Chile under Allende and France under Mitterrand. Resistance by businesses and the wealthy created economic disorder that either forced the government to retreat or resulted in a military coup. Political movements that promise to make changes that benefit people in the bottom half of the income distribution lose significant parts of their political support when the economy is disrupted by inflation, higher unemployment, or shortages. Drawing on the analysis of earlier chapters, I shall argue that a democratizing habitation strategy has advantages over other strategies on both of these dimensions.

POLITICAL ADVANTAGES

The present period of intense political polarization has similarities to the 1930s when fascist paramilitaries clashed with communist and socialist militants in the streets of various countries. Both then and now, both sides perceive the victory of the other as an existential threat. Trump, for example, rallies his supporters by insisting that his Democratic opponents are socialists and communists determined to use the state to impose their multicultural values through coercion. At the same time, Trump's opponents are deeply fearful that he will emulate Vladimir Putin and create an authoritarian regime in which dissidents are routinely imprisoned and protests would be outlawed.

At one level, these fears are not irrational since both left-wing and right-wing regimes have systematically violated human rights. Nevertheless, it is still striking how far removed these fears are from the disagreements that are typical in periods of normal politics. Those standard left–right disputes center on how large a role the government should play in society, the appropriate level of taxation, and how active the government should be in redistributing income and wealth. But with polarization, those disputes tend to fade into the background because both left-wing and right-wing movements embrace an expansion of the government's role and favor some types of redistribution.[7]

These existential fears associated with polarization are, in fact, far removed from everyday pocketbook issues like the cost of living or the state of the labor market. Nevertheless, we saw during the Covid pandemic, how easily political polarization spilled over into everyday questions such as whether one should wear a mask, be vaccinated, or take a veterinary medication—ivermectin—to combat coronavirus. In fact, there is evidence that after the vaccine was made available, excess deaths caused by Covid were substantially higher in predominantly Republican counties than in Democratic counties.[8]

This fact indicates the difficulty of reducing the polarization and returning to something that more closely resembles normal political disagreements. In the earlier period of extreme polarization, it took a world war to defeat fascism and return it to the margins of political life. It seems unlikely that two, three, or even five years of stable economic growth will be enough to detach current followers from the far-right leaders that they see as providing the most promising protection from the threatened authoritarianism of the left. This is especially the case because the media apparatus that creates and amplifies these fears is unlikely to shift to less polarizing messages.

It follows that most strategies of the left have a high probability of intensifying the polarization with little chance of reaching a tipping point where support for the far-right diminishes. For example, the Biden Administration has been more aggressive than any Democratic Administration since the New Deal in pursuing policies that benefit white working-class people. Nevertheless, even after more than three years, Republican politicians both at the state level and at the national level remain firmly attached to Donald Trump and his MAGA movement. Had the Biden Administration embraced even more of the policies of the Congressional Progressive Caucus including "common sense" gun reforms, forgiving of student loans, and more generous support for the care economy, the right-wing backlash might have been even stronger.

The democratizing habitation strategy is not a magic cure to end polarization. In fact, we can expect that its initiatives would immediately be demonized by right-wing media as yet another face of the left's totalitarian agenda. However, there are several elements to the strategy that have the potential to diminish polarization. First, the strategy is focused on giving people at the local level more power and control over the immediate conditions of their life. This represents an important shift from the left's focus since the civil rights movement on using the power of the federal government to enhance the rights of African Americans, women, immigrants, and sexual minorities. Since the right has historically opposed increasing the power of the federal government, some of its adherents could be drawn to a movement focused on empowering localities.[9]

Second, the focus of a movement to democratize habitation on concrete issues such as expanding affordable housing and increasing resilience in the face of extreme weather events has the potential to bypass the differences created by polarization. A Trump-supporting neighbor is likely to share an interest in keeping flood waters away and might be willing to work with people on the other side. Moreover, as people work together on common goals, there is an opportunity for conversations and friendships to reduce polarization.

Third, the strategy of democratizing habitation depends on a significant expansion of the resources available to subnational governments, so that win-win solutions can be found for ongoing conflicts. For example, addressing housing affordability in cities usually requires increasing density, and this is often seen as a threat to neighborhoods of single-family homes. However, there can be win-win solutions in which higher density buildings are concentrated on heavily trafficked streets which are then also used for light rail or buses. People in the residential neighborhoods get to keep their single-family homes, but they gain access to more convenient mass transit options. The search for compromises in which benefits are shared can keep conflicts from feeding polarization. Democratizing habitation also requires that neighborhoods that were historically segregated and deprived of quality services be upgraded, but with access to new funding this would be less likely to stir resentment.

Fourth, much of the most intense political polarization has been between large cities and rural areas and small towns. Across the U.S., Donald Trump carried rural counties often with 80 per cent of the vote, while almost every large city in the nation votes heavily Democratic. There is a material explanation for this divergence. While rural counties receive more benefits from both the federal and state governments than they pay in taxes, they have suffered economic marginalization in recent decades. Their share of total population has declined steadily over many decades, and they often lack quality education and medical care. Moreover, many rural areas have not had access to broadband or cell phone coverage, and employment opportunities have fallen with both plant closings and the decline of family farms. This has fueled resentment that has been channeled into support for MAGA Republicans.

However, the politics of democratizing habitation involves developing cooperative relationships between urban and rural areas as a way to improve habitation in both types of communities. Efforts to provide rural areas with high-speed broadband and cellular service would be accelerated, and rural healthcare and education would receive additional support. New financing arrangements would open up greater possibilities for rural entrepreneurs. Open space in rural areas would be used to create wind farms and large solar arrays that generate revenue for people in those areas and electrical power for the more densely populated locales. Systematic efforts would be made at the state or provincial level to subsidize the preservation of open space in rural counties to create employment opportunities around tourism and recreation. Subsidies might also be used to revive small-scale agriculture that is environmentally sound.

While rural–urban polarization is not likely to disappear quickly, efforts like this could diminish its intensity and quite possibly reverse the population decline in a significant number of localities. In contrast to other political initiatives, there is a chance that an increasing number of people in rural areas would recognize that democratizing habitation is a political strategy that responds to their interests and needs.

ECONOMIC ADVANTAGES

The analysis of investment in Chapter 5 helps to explain why the strategy of democratizing habitation is economically sound. I showed there that the bulk of productive investment each year is done by government and communities, households and non-profits, rather than by businesses. The focus in democratizing habitation is to expand the resources available to government, households, and non-profits so they would increase their productive investments. Moreover, their increased outlays would tend to concentrate on infrastructure, clean energy, and those intangible investments in care and community building that make the economy more productive without increasing the burden on the already stressed environment.

At the same time, the new financing structures described in Chapter 6 would strengthen cooperative network production that would expand the economic role of small and medium-sized enterprises. This would help to accelerate the rate of innovation as compared to an economy dominated by giant corporations. We noted earlier that large corporations often buy up startups with the intention of killing an innovation that might threaten their own markets. With new financing institutions, those new firms would have a better chance of surviving. Moreover, as these alternative financial institutions displaced the existing ones, the flow of funds into largely speculative investments such as derivatives and cryptocurrency would diminish. More of society's capital would be available for meeting the challenge of climate change and raising the capacities of the population.

Democratizing habitation will necessarily involve raising more revenue through taxation. The U.S. ratio of tax to GDP—as it is currently measured by the BEA—was 26.6 per cent in 2021, well below the average for OECD countries of 34.1 per cent. The actual gap is even more substantial given that the U.S. spends so much more on defense and national security than other nations. Given that democratizing habitation involves substantially increased public spending on infrastructure, clean energy, conservation, affordable housing, education, research and development, support for various forms of care, and managing the urban–rural divide, this cannot be done without a substantial increase in tax revenue.

This increase in taxation would have to be phased in over a decade. In the shorter term, some of the needed revenue can be raised by clawing back some of the vast wealth acquired over the past 40 years by the top 1 per cent of households. This could be done by closing loopholes that benefit the extremely rich and implementing the kind of wealth tax proposed by Elizabeth Warren.[10] If a wealth tax proved unfeasible, the other option would be to require people in higher income brackets to pay taxes on unrealized capital gains on stock ownership. This would put an end to the practice where some of the billionaires earn almost no income, but rather borrow funds to cover their expenses using their huge financial portfolios as collateral.

However, it would also be necessary to increase broad-based taxation by creating a value added tax (VAT) on both goods and services. The European experience is that VAT raises considerable revenue and generates relatively little political resistance.[11] Moreover, the potentially regressive impact of a consumption tax can be offset by more generous policies towards the poor. Initially the VAT could be introduced at a low rate such as 5 per cent with complicated formulas to compensate states and localities for the loss of sales tax revenues, but over a decade, the patchwork of different local sales taxes would be replaced with a substantially higher, but uniform federal VAT that was combined with more generous revenue sharing with state and local governments.

Claims that this higher tax burden relative to GDP would hurt the economy rest on the mistaken argument that business investment is the key to economic prosperity. In fact, a large share of the increased government spending would consist of investment outlays designed to expand the economy's capacity to produce. They would, in turn, likely lead to increase in investments by businesses, households, and non-profits. Moreover, as citizens began to experience improved habitation while also having a greater voice in how funds were being allocated at the state and local level, their distaste for taxation would likely diminish.

THE TRANSITION TROUGH

The democratizing habitation approach also has the potential to circumvent one of the major obstacles to radical reform initiatives. Historically when leftist governments are elected with a radical agenda, business interests have sabotaged the economy by withholding investment (capital strikes) and shifting funds abroad (capital flight). While the left party had won elections based on promises to improve the life situation of people in the bottom half of the income distribution, the capital strikes and capital flight hurt those same people through unemployment and declining purchasing power of the currency. This is what Erik Olin Wright referred to as the transition trough in moving to a post-capitalist economy.[12] The longer and deeper the trough, the greater the likelihood that the elected government will either retreat from its radical agenda or be thrown out of office.

However, the democratizing habitation strategy has the potential to make the transition trough shallower and shorter by building institutional power before provoking a major confrontation with entrenched interests. In the first phase of the strategy, probably lasting for ten years, the focus would be on expanding the resources available to local communities and giving residents greater influence over their habitation. Much of the emphasis would be on climate change, housing affordability, and racial justice. A major priority in this phase would be building powerful networks of non-profit financial institutions that would grow alongside the existing financial system.[13]

As discussed in Chapter 6, the central government could be pressured into helping to create this network of non-profit financial institutions. The government would provide start-up capital and loan guarantees to expand this network of lenders that would then provide low-cost loans for infrastructure projects, for clean energy, for affordable housing, and to support non-profit services.

More confrontational policies towards the wealthy and entrenched corporations would happen in the second phase of the strategy. But at this point, the strategy's opponents would find that the effectiveness of capital strike and capital flight had diminished. Private sector investment is already less important than public and community investment. At this future moment, any deliberate decline in private sector investment could easily be offset by greater public sector spending and increased lending to households, non-profits, and the public sector. Furthermore, both the Federal Reserve and the non-profit banks would be able to increase foreign borrowing to reduce the impact of capital flight. These measures could make the transition trough both shallow and brief. With continued public support, the path would be open to impose tighter regulations on large firms and for-profit financial institutions.

The goal, in short, would be to establish firm democratic control over the entire economy. The pursuit of private profit would likely continue for some time. However, profit-making firms would be subject to tighter regulations designed to block predatory behavior and to make them more responsive to consumer needs. They would also be required to include employees in both decision-making and the sharing of profits. Moreover, effective competition would be restored in many market niches both through financial arrangements that strengthened small and medium-sized enterprises and by the growth of public and non-profit businesses. The now dominant internet firms would likely be regulated as public utilities, but with greater democratic safeguards to prevent regulatory capture by the businesses. The big challenge here is to establish a more democratic mode of corporate and business regulation that would reduce the opportunities for entrenched interests to capture the regulatory agencies.[14]

EMPLOYEE EMPOWERMENT

Since most of us work at producing habitation, the project of democratizing habitation necessarily requires giving employees greater voice at the workplace. However, given the huge variation in workplaces in size, in type of organization, in level of employee commitment, and in the role of expert knowledge, there is no "one-size-fits-all" version of a democratic workplace. Although new financing arrangements would afford much more opportunity in the economy for cooperatives and employee-owned firms that could be organized in a radically democratic fashion,[15] this would not work for public sector organizations whose direction and policies are substantially shaped by elected officials. Nor would it make sense for small businesses, many non-profits, and profit-oriented corporations.

Nevertheless, there are a wide range of different policies and mechanisms that could expand employee voice across all types of employment. One indispensable step is to radically diminish the share of the workforce who are vulnerable to arbitrary dismissal because they are defined as "at-will" employees. Virtually everyone who has been at a job through a six-month probationary period should be entitled to due process before being fired. This step, in itself, would significantly reduce the arbitrary power of employers and make it possible for employees to exert more collective pressure on management. A related measure is to reduce dramatically the ability of firms to pretend that their employees are "independent contractors" who therefore have no rights at all in the workplace.

Another key step is to legally mandate that all organizations above a certain size be required to create a works council elected by employees that is empowered to meet regularly with management and is given access to key information about the organization. The experience of such works councils in Germany suggests that this institutional arrangement promotes a more collaborative relation between employer and employees while also helping firms be more productive. At a later stage, a further reform would allow employees in privately owned firms to elect representatives to the firm's board of directors.[16]

Finally, since works councils are primarily focused on cooperative relations between employees and employers, there is also a pressing need to increase the ability of employees to push back against management through unions. However, in both the U.S. and the U.K., union density—the portion of the workforce enrolled in unions—has been falling for years as employers use both legal and illegal tactics to defeat organizing campaigns. Labor law reforms are urgently needed to keep employers from using tactics such as firings, delay, and captive audience meetings as a way to resist unionization campaigns.

All of these are expedients intended to reverse the current managerial tendency to see employees as expendable and easily replaced inputs who should be compensated as cheaply as possible. Across all workplaces, employees need and deserve a voice in how the organization works in order to produce the highest quality outputs.

THE GLOBAL DIMENSION

The project of democratizing habitation in individual nations will only be successful if there is also significant progress towards changing the institutions and rules that currently govern the global economy. These rules and institutions currently work to reinforce the mistaken mainstream orthodoxy that sees business investment as the key to economic prosperity. Governments that attempt to pursue heterodox policies are usually punished with intensified speculation against their currencies and higher borrowing costs when selling government bonds.

Nevertheless, there are multiple reasons to believe that significant reforms of the global economic order are feasible in the short term. There is an emerging global consensus that the long reign of market liberalism or neoliberalism has been an abject failure both in raising standards of living and dealing with climate change. Market liberalism and lax regulation of the financial system were obviously causes of the global financial crisis in 2008–09 that could have easily produced a replay of the global depression of the 1930s. But once a global collapse had been averted, there was a return to economic orthodoxy in which governments were pressured to prioritize balanced budgets. The result was ten years of below average economic growth. In contrast, the successful use of government spending to manage the massive economic consequences of the Covid pandemic has forced second thoughts. Moreover, the supply chain disruptions caused by Covid have forced governments to reconsider the benefits and risks of moving production to offshore locations.

While the United States has been the main architect and defender of the existing global economic order, the Biden Administration has clearly indicated its rejection of some important parts of the previous economic orthodoxy. This is evident in the open embrace of industrial policy in the Inflation Reduction Act and the Chips and Science Act.[17] Through the use of government loans, tax credits, subsidies for research and development, and domestic content rules, the U.S. government is in clear violation of the old global norms that governments should not favor domestic production over imports from abroad. Moreover, the U.S. has responded to complaints by telling its allies that they should embrace a comparable set of industrial policies. The U.S. has also indicated its interest in larger global change by strongly pushing the World

Bank to dramatically increase its lending to combat climate change and support resilience.

Furthermore, the existential threat of rising temperatures and weather-related disasters has also made it obvious that international economic arrangements must be restructured to facilitate much higher levels of spending around the world to both combat climate change and protect populations from its consequences. This is evident in the U.S. push to expand World Bank lending, but even more radical steps are needed to accelerate investments to protect populations from climate change and to reduce greenhouse gases.

Finally, there are geopolitical reasons to reform the global economic order. As in the 1930s, the pressures of the global economy have been a significant element in fueling authoritarian turns in multiple countries. Moreover, a tighter alliance between Russia and China could become the lynchpin of a global coalition of authoritarian powers that would increase the threat of broader military conflicts. A revised global economic architecture could defuse some of these dangers since it would acknowledge China's rise as a global economic power and diminish the United States's ability to exercise its power without constraint.

For all these reasons, global economic reform ideas that have been debated for decades have a better chance of implementation.[18] The first critical step is to implement a version of the international clearing union that Keynes proposed in the 1940s. This could happen with relatively modest reforms within the International Monetary Fund (IMF). Keynes's core idea was that global liquidity would be provided by a global currency issued by an international body. This meant that the growth of global money could be managed collectively rather than being dependent on new supplies of gold or the decisions of central bankers to increase their holdings of reserve currencies such as the dollar or the euro. Moreover, Keynes envisioned that his international clearing union would operate as a lender of last resort so that nations having balance of payments difficulties would not have to impose austerity policies that included higher levels of unemployment.

In fact, the IMF created this kind of global currency already in the 1970s by establishing special drawing rights (SDRs) that were the equivalent of global money. However, new issues of SDRs stopped in 1981 until the program was suddenly revived in the middle of the global financial crisis in 2009. At that time, $161.2 billion worth of SDRs were allocated to IMF members to counteract the global economic downturn. Then again, the program was dormant until the Fund distributed $456.5 billion worth of SDRs in 2021 to help governments contend with the economic dislocations created by the Covid pandemic. Proposals have been made, but not yet implemented for another large-scale issuance of SDRs to accelerate government actions to combat climate change.

A decision to begin allocating a significant quantity of SDRs on an annual basis would be an important step in reducing the bias towards austerity in the existing global order. Over recent decades, governments have accumulated huge reserves of currencies in order to protect themselves from speculation against their currencies. Globally, those reserves were worth almost $12 trillion in 2022. With access to SDRs and greater ability to rely on IMF resources, governments could begin to draw down those reserves to spend them on climate resilience and clean energy.

The increased use of SDRs would begin to reduce the dollar's central role in the global economy. This would help defuse some of the current tensions between China and the United States and put pressure on the U.S. to pull back from its unsustainable global network of military bases. It would also diminish the inflow of funds from around the world to Wall Street that fuel various speculative investments.

A second reform would be to introduce a global financial transaction tax that would significantly dampen the current level of trading in the foreign exchange markets and various derivative instruments. Daily transactions in foreign currencies have reached a level of $5 trillion. This is vastly more than required to pay for trade, investments, remittances, and tourism. The trading tends to be profitable because transaction costs are low and most currencies follow relatively predictable trend lines. However, this volume of trading unleashes vast speculative pressures on nations that deviate from market orthodoxy. The combination of SDRs and a financial transaction tax would help expand the economic policy space available to governments.

This, in turn, would make it substantially easier to pursue the agenda of democratizing habitation.

RESTRUCTURING AT THE LOCAL LEVEL

The reforms proposed at the national, supranational, and global levels are all designed to facilitate more effective democratic governance at the local level so that people in cities, suburbs, small towns, and rural communities would have a much greater ability to shape their own habitation. This would happen through several distinct mechanisms:

1. Increased regulation and greater competition would make businesses providing financial services, medical services, housing, utilities, and other goods and services more responsive to their consumers.
2. Subnational governments would have more resources to fund the clean energy transition, build infrastructure and affordable housing, and create a much stronger and better care economy including childcare, a variety of health services, education, and eldercare.
3. Small businesses, cooperatives, and non-profits would have more access to resources to provide vital community amenities.
4. Voters would have an enhanced ability to pressure local officials to improve the quality of government services and to assure greater fairness across different neighborhoods.

Achieving this will involve experimentation with a range of different mechanisms to revitalize and strengthen democratic participation in subnational governments. For example, cities around the world have experimented with participatory budgeting to give residents a greater voice in how spending should be allocated. However, these initiatives differ radically in the share of the budget that residents can influence and the degree to which implementation continues to be shaped by their input. However, the experiments demonstrate the possibility of involving large numbers of people when there are significant resources at stake.[19]

Other mechanisms of greater citizen participation include the use of citizen assemblies or citizen juries that operate on the same kind of principle as trial juries and grand juries. A random group of citizens are assembled to study a particular topic, such as different options for citing a major infrastructure project. Participants are paid to deliberate for a limited period of time, during which they can question experts with different perspectives. After thorough discussion, they vote on what they think is the best option.[20] Moreover, citizen juries can be used to frame referenda, so that voters could have the opportunity to choose among alternative proposals.

Another possibility is to use elected boards to give citizens more influence over governmental decisions. While strongly resisted by police unions, some cities have created elected civilian review boards that can process investigate episodes of racist or otherwise problematic police behavior. Similar boards could be created for healthcare, childcare, or to oversee agencies that handle landlord–tenant conflicts.

These mechanisms could work to increase the influence of people over governmental institutions without running into the problem of too many time-consuming meetings.[21] Effective democratization does not require everyone to stay up-to-date on all of the local issues and develop a sophisticated understanding of how politics works. But it does require many more people to become informal community leaders as they develop knowledge and the ability to persuade their neighbors to vote or participate in some other kind of political action. Moreover, it seems highly likely that as local governments gain control over more economic resources, more of these trusted informal leaders will emerge.

There is, however, a danger that this locally-based political strategy could exacerbate existing patterns of inequality, particularly along racial lines. Central government institutions, including particularly the court system, would need to monitor local developments to assure that these newly acquired local resources were being used to alleviate rather than intensify inequalities across different racial and ethnic groups and across different neighborhoods. Those mobilizing to democratize habitation would have to prioritize the disciplining of those localities that refused to pursue policies that are equalizing and inclusive.

There would also need to be experimentation with new mechanisms of metropolitan governance to manage the relationship among cities, poorer suburbs, and richer suburbs. We are already seeing voters in richer suburbs resisting the building of affordable housing in their communities. Moreover, more affluent suburbs are often able to spend more per pupil in their schools. A series of reforms will be necessary to break the pattern in which more affluent communities are able to wall themselves off from the concerns and needs of their less affluent neighbors.

CONCLUSION

The argument developed here is that a strategy of democratizing habitation is a sensible and reasonable response to the lived reality of contemporary developed societies. The strategy has the potential to create solidarity across a wide range of different constituencies and it would significantly improve the well-being of much of the population. But while I have tried to show that the strategy is a response to very real ongoing economic changes, there is no historical force pushing in this direction. On the contrary, our present reality is that oligarchic power is subverting democratic institutions at the national level while lower levels of government lack the resources and capabilities to improve most people's habitation.

The strategy of democratizing habitation requires many people to organize and mobilize around this agenda. But the hope is that if such a movement were to win some small initial reforms, it would have a transformative effect by showing that people really can reshape their habitation through collective action. The old mantra of community organizers is that you start by fighting for something that is winnable, such as a traffic light at a dangerous intersection. When people taste a small victory, such as being able to cross a street safely, it whets their appetite for more. The victory can give rise to rent strikes against predatory landlords and broader mobilizations to demand more affordable housing.

Once people recognize that they do not have to accept the ugly tradeoffs that most of us experience in contemporary societies, including unaffordable housing, significant homeless populations, lousy and expensive care options for infants, children, and the elderly, and routine mistreatment by predatory corporations, they can begin to imagine a different kind of society. Think, for example, of living in a community where poverty and homelessness did not exist because everyone was provided access to housing, food, and healthcare. Imagine that crime and substance abuse were far less common because many fewer people were living lives of quiet desperation. Consider that when new technologies such as robots and AI were introduced, they would not lead to unemployment and increased job insecurity for millions, but rather reduced workweeks for those who wanted them. Or ponder that instead of Elon Musk accumulating a fortune of $215 billion, that $214 of those billions were used to improve the care services available to every person.

In short, when most of us produce habitation and all of us consume habitation, a better world is possible. In that better world, we could meet the existential challenge of climate change. We could address the deepening gap between standards of living in the developed world and the developing world. We could address the current crisis of global migration by attacking the causes that drive people to risk everything to escape violence, poverty, and drought to get to North America, Europe, or Australia. We could also prove, once and for all, that democracies are better than autocracies. In a word, the democratization of habitation will not occur unless lots of people organize and mobilize around this agenda. While nothing is guaranteed, one thing does seem certain. Democratic and egalitarian movements that continue to rely on the economic analyses and economic remedies developed in the industrial era are bound to fail. Too much has changed for the recycling of hundred-year-old slogans to be politically effective. We are living in an entirely different world than the one inhabited by our grandparents and great grandparents. Without new political strategies and new rhetoric, we cannot meet the challenges of this historical moment.

Notes

1 ACCOUNTING FOR MORBID SYMPTOMS

1. Hoare & Nowell Smith, *Selections from the Prison Notebooks of Antonio Gramsci*, 276.
2. This line of argument builds on Karl Polanyi's diagnosis of the rise of fascism in *The Great Transformation*; see, e.g., Rabinowitz, *Defensive Nationalism*; see also Block & Somers, *The Power of Market Fundamentalism*.
3. Piketty, *Capital and Ideology*; see also Kitschelt & Rehm, "Polarity reversal."
4. Mudge, *Leftism Reinvented*.
5. Crotty, *Keynes Against Capitalism*.
6. A Brookings study estimated that in 2020, 77 per cent of jobs in the U.S. were characterized by high or moderate levels of digitalization; see Muro and Liu, "As the digitalization of work expands, place-based solutions can bridge the gaps".
7. Block, "Read their lips: taxation and the right wing agenda."
8. Bell, *The Coming of Postindustrial Society*. Others who developed these ideas include Brzezinski, *Between two Ages*; Touraine, *The Post-Industrial Society*; Toffler, *Future Shock*; Calvert and Neiman, *A Disrupted History*.
9. In 1977, there were 18.7 gallons of whole cow's milk for each person in the U.S. By 2017, this had fallen to 5.7 gallons: https://www.ers.usda.gov/data-products/chart-gallery/gallery/chart-detail/?chartId=96991.
10. In the national income and product accounts, homeowners are treated as though they are renting their homes and even when a household finances the construction of a new home, it is counted as an investment expenditure by the business sector.

2 WHY HABITATION?

1. A similar project uses the concept of the foundational economy. See The Foundational Economy Collective, *The Foundational Economy*. The group has a website: https://foundationaleconomy.com/.

2. Polanyi does not provide a citation for this pamphlet, but it is "A Consideration of the Cause in Question before the Lords touching Depopulation." It is cited in Gay, "The Midland Revolt of 1607".
3. Parliament did eventually enact limits on child labor and on the length of the working day in response to protests and public backlash against what William Blake had labeled the "dark Satanic Mills" of early industrialism.
4. Schumpeter, *Capitalism, Socialism and Democracy*.
5. Polanyi develops this distinction most clearly in "The Economy as Instituted Process." In making this distinction, Polanyi drew on Max Weber's analysis of formal and substantive rationality. The former was the result of following a specific set of rules or procedures, while the latter involved a holistic evaluation of possible outcomes. Weber's insight was that formal rationality could produce substantive irrationality.
6. The political philosopher, Nancy Fraser, has drawn on these Polanyian insights to revise and deepen the Marxist critique of capitalism; see Fraser, "Can society be commodities all the way down?" and "Crisis of care?".
7. Jacob Hacker focuses on this variable in *The Great Risk Shift*.
8. Smith, *The Theory of Moral Sentiments* and *The Wealth of Nations*. For a recent argument that Adam Smith was not a market fundamentalist thinker, see Anderson, *Hijacked*, ch. 5. For further elaboration of the moral critique, see Block, *Capitalism*, ch. 4.
9. Cato Institute, 2022 Housing Affordability National Survey; https://www.cato.org/survey-reports/poll-87-americans-worry-about-cost-housing-69-worry-their-kids-grandkids-wont-be#.
10. AAPA/The Harris Poll, *The Patient Experience*.
11. KFF, "KFF survey on affordability of long-term care and support service."
12. Morning Consult, "State of childcare in the United States."
13. Pew Research Center, "Inflation, health costs, partisan cooperation among the nation's top problems."
14. Cox, D. *et al*. "Public places and commercial spaces". This American Community Life survey happened during the peak period of Covid-19 so some of the discontent might have been intensified by the pandemic.
15. Tyson, Funk & Kennedy, "What the data says about Americans' views of climate change."
16. Smarth Growth America/Hattaway Communications, *American Attitudes on Transportation Spending*. This is a survey designed to shift public opinion away from support for highway construction.
17. See footnote 8, Chapter 1.
18. The ideas and influence of the free-market theorists are addressed in a large literature that includes Mirowski & Plehwe (eds), *The Road from Mont Pelerin*; Burgin, *The Great Persuasion*; and Slobodian, *Globalists*.
19. In reality, however, "free market" policies often involved an increase in governmental coercion. For example, welfare programs were made contingent on work requirements that were then enforced by public sector workers who were empowered to cut off assistance. In other words, while free-market theorists attack their opponents for relying on government,

realizing their own policy agenda can only be done with the help of governmental power; Block & Somers, *The Power of Market Fundamentalism*.
20. Rich, *Think Tanks, Public Policy and the Politics of Expertise*.
21. Mizruchi, *The Fracturing of the American Corporate Elite*.
22. Block, Keller & Negoita, "Revisiting the hidden developmental state."
23. Schrank & Whitford, "The anatomy of network failure" and Whitford & Schrank, "The paradox of the weak state revisited."
24. Block, "Swimming against the current," 188.
25. Keller & Block, "Explaining the transformation in the U.S. innovation system."
26. Block & Keller, *State of Innovation*.
27. OECD, "Population with tertiary education"; https://data.oecd.org/eduatt/population-with-tertiary-education.htm.
28. Gemici, "Beyond the Minsky and Polanyi moments."

3 COMMODIFICATION WITHOUT COMMODITIES

1. It does not make sense, however, to label all of these things as fictitious commodities. I would reserve that term for land, labor, money, and knowledge—all of which are not produced for sale on a market. I am suggesting instead a tripartite distinction. There are fictitious commodities, problematic commodities, and classical commodities—the standardized products that are provided by multiple suppliers and that are transferred in a single moment in time.
2. Note that most legal work is either done on behalf of businesses or paid for by government agencies. Hence, legal work represents a very small share of personal consumption expenditures.
3. Colleen Dunlavy shows that the standardization of manufactured goods that occurred in the U.S. between the 1920s and 1950s was largely driven by governmental initiatives in the 1920s. The government, led by Secretary of Commerce, Herbert Hoover, understood that firms would only be able to take advantage of mass production technologies if they ceased offering a bewildering variety of products; Dunlavy, *Small, Medium, Large*.
4. McDonough & Braungart, *Cradle to Cradle*.
5. In the U.K., Margaret Thatcher's Right to Buy policy that gave tenants the option of purchasing council housing has helped create an acute shortage of affordable housing.
6. Molotch, "The city as a growth machine."
7. Epstein, *Impure Science*.
8. Hoyert, "Maternal morality rates in the United States 2021."
9. McGee, *The Sum of Us*.

4 THE IRONY OF CORPORATE DOMINANCE

1. The standard account of the rise of these firms is Chandler, *Scale and Scope*.
2. Block, "Financial democratization and the transition to socialism."
3. Examples of fanciful or fraudulent innovation include Elizabeth Holmes'

health technology company Theranos and Sam Bankman-Fried's cryptocurrency exchange FTX. Purdue Pharma's innovation was to make the painkiller OxyContin available in a 12-hour time-release capsule. This innovation made it easy for users to modify the pill to get the 12-hour dose immediately. This resulted in addiction and a search by addicts for other opiates.

4. Gertner, *The Idea Factory*.
5. Block & Keller, "Where do innovations come from?"
6. Jacobs, *Short-term America*.
7. Block, Keller & Negoita, "Revisiting the hidden developmental state."
8. Bonvillian & Singer, *Advanced Manufacturing*.
9. Most of the information on the helmet challenge is drawn from the NFL's own website; see also McMichael, "3 next-gen helmet designs that could curb concussions in the NFL."
10. Whitford & Schrank, "The paradox of the weak state"; Schrank & Whitford, "The anatomy of network failure."
11. Brandt & Whitford, "Fixing network failures."
12. National Research Council, *Funding a Revolution*.
13. American Automotive Policy Council, *State of the U.S. Automotive Industry, 2020*.
14. Womack, Jones & Roos, *The Machine that Changed the World*.
15. Johns Hopkins Bloomburg School of Public Health, "Cost of clinical trials for new drug FDA approval are fraction of total tab."
16. Dayen, "Amazon continues preying on third-party sellers."
17. Berk & Saxenian, "Rethinking antitrust for the cloud era."
18. The classic account of Taylorism is Braverman, *Labor and Monopoly Capital*.
19. Fisk, *Working Knowledge*.
20. Gray & Suri, *Ghost Work*.
21. Berger, *Making in America*.
22. Smith & Alexander, *Fumbling the Future*.
23. Kidder, *The Soul of a New Machine*.
24. Lester & Piore, *Innovation*.
25. Kulish, Kliff & Silver-Greenberg, "The U.S. tried to build a new fleet of ventilators."
26. Wikipedia.

5   WHAT COUNTS AS INVESTMENT?

1. Hassett, "Investment." Both the goods used for production and the goods that are produced can be both tangible and intangible. A software program is an intangible investment and its output could be something intangible such as a strategy for trading stocks.
2. More precisely, government spending other than those expenditures that are counted as investment.
3. Mazzucato, *The Value of Everything*.
4. Folbre, "The unproductive housewife."

5. Christophers, *Banking Across Borders*.
6. Kuhn, *The Structure of Scientific Revolutions*.
7. Calculating depreciation is so difficult because different capital goods deteriorate at very different rates, and analysts are forced to estimate average service lives based on surveys. Moreover, it is particularly difficult to estimate the service lives of intangible investments such as expenditures for computer software, research and development, or outlays to upgrade the skills and capabilities of workers. Surprisingly, there is remarkably little economic literature on the difficulty of calculating depreciation of intangible assets. For a typical treatment, see Haskel & Westlake, *Capitalism without Capital*, 56–7.
8. Piketty, *Capital in the Twenty-First Century*, 119.
9. Bourdieu, "The forms of capital;" Putnam, *Bowling Alone*.
10. Crotty, *Keynes Against Capitalism*.
11. Solow, "Technical change and the aggregate production function."
12. Schultz, "Investment in human capital."
13. Denison, *Accounting for Economic Growth, 1929–1969*; Kendrick, *The Formation and Stocks of Total Capital*; Eisner, *The Total Income System of Accounts*.
14. BEA, "Improved estimates of the National Income and Product Accounts for 1959–95."
15. Parker & Grimm, "Recognition of business and government expenditures for software as investment."
16. Soloveichik & Wasshausen, "Copyright-protected assets in the National Accounts."
17. Corrado, Hulten & Sichel, "Measuring capital and technology;" Corrado, Hulten & Sichel, "Intangible capital and U.S. economic growth;" see also the later study by Haskel & Westlake, *Capitalism*.
18. Landefeld, Villones & Holdren, "GDP and beyond."
19. Abraham & Mallatt, "Measuring human capital."
20. *Ibid*.
21. Jorgenson & Fraumeni, "The output of the education sector."
22. Abraham & Mallatt, "Measuring human capital."
23. A number of economists argue that spending by businesses for marketing and branding and for creating distinctive business models should also be counted as intangible investment; see Haskel & Westlake, *Capitalism*. This would mean that outlays for design of products, advertising, and management consultants would count as investment. I find this argument unpersuasive since these expenditures are generally intended to improve a firm's market share relative to competitors rather than increase overall output.
24. Kuhn, *Structure of Scientific Revolutions*.
25. Toupin, *Wages for Housework*.
26. Vogel, *Marxism and the Oppression of Women*; see also Bhattacharya, *Social Reproduction Theory*.
27. Folbre, *For Love or Money*; Fraser, "Can society be commodities all the way down?" and "Crisis of care?".
28. Barbara Ehrenreich analyzes familiar arguments that welfare spending is

bad because it encourages dependence. She then goes on to show that this privileging of independence over dependence requires ignoring that human beings come into the world and leave it dependent on others; Ehrenreich, "The new right attack on social welfare."
29. Folbre & Heintz, "Investment, consumption, or public good?;" Heintz, "Public investments and human investments."
30. Fraser, "Commodities all the way down."
31. Kenworthy, *Social Democratic Capitalism*.
32. Morel, Palier & Palme (eds), *Towards a Social Investment Welfare State?*; Hemerijck, *The Uses of Social Investment*; Garritzmann, Häusermann & Palier, *The World Politics of Social Investment*, vols I & II; Hemerijck, Ronchi & Plavgo, "Social investment as a conceptual framework for analyzing well-being and reforms in the 21st century."
33. Häusermann, Garritzmann & Palier, "The politics of social investment."
34. Kenworthy, *Social Democratic Capitalism*.
35. Many of the largest non-profits such as private universities and hospital chains are often managed in ways that are quite similar to profit-seeking corporations. However, non-profits are subject to a tighter regulatory framework than corporations, and those regulations could be used to force non-profits to behave differently than their corporate counterparts.
36. See Hendren & Sprung-Keyser, "A unified welfare analysis of government policies."
37. It follows as well that transfers to older people such as social security are not included as investments even though some recipients might be doing childcare or passing on skills to younger people.
38. Congressional Budget Office, "Fair-value estimates of the cost of federal credit programs in 2019."
39. Keynes, *The General Theory of Employment, Interest, and Money*, 378.
40. Crotty, *Keynes Against Capitalism*.
41. Block & Keller, *State of Innovation*; Mazzucato, *The Entrepreneurial State*.
42. It is relevant that bills passed in 2022 in the U.S. significantly increased the use of tax credits and loan guarantees to encourage private sector investments that would address climate change and U.S. production of computer chips; Keller & Block, "The new levers of state power."
43. Abraham & Mallatt, "Measuring human capital."
44. Rama, "National health expenditures, 2018: spending growth remains steady even with increases in private health insurance and Medicare spending."
45. Childcare Aware of America, "The US and the high price of child care."
46. Detailed price data are provided by Landivar, Graf & Rayo, "Childcare prices in local areas."
47. The Bureau of Labor Statistics estimates that only 11 per cent of employees have access to employer-sponsored childcare; Bipartisan Policy Center, "Childcare is a business affair."
48. The $14,000 a year figure might seem high as an average expenditure. However, I use that figure because this calculation leaves out two key areas of expense. More affluent families hire nannies who can be paid $30 an

hour ($60,000 per year), and many families pay for after-school care for children aged between six and ten. Hence, the total childcare figure here is a conservative estimate.
49. Suh & Folbre, "Valuing unpaid child care in the U.S."
50. OECD Family Database, "Public spending on family benefits."
51. My argument is that the BEA estimates of the depreciation of government investment—both tangible and intangible—are too high. Some of the reasons have been spelled out. An additional problem is that the BEA calculates depreciation in the national income accounts at replacement cost rather than historical cost. This choice significantly increases depreciation, especially since in an ever-changing economy, many of those older assets will not be replaced by comparable equipment. Think, for example, of the replacement cost of aging nuclear power plants that will ultimately be replaced by far cheaper wind and solar energy.
52. Freiberger & Swaine, *Fire in the Valley*.

6 DYSFUNCTIONAL FINANCING

1. Newfield, *The Great Mistake*; Goldin & Katz, *The Race Between Education and Technology*.
2. Allegretto, "The teacher pay penalty has hit a new high."
3. ASCE, "Infrastructure investment gap 2020–2029."
4. Congressional Research Service, "A visual depiction of the shift from defined benefit (DB) to defined contribution (DC) pension plans in the private sector."
5. Braun, "Exit, control, and politics."
6. Butler & Germanis, "Achieving social security reform."
7. Palladino & Lazonick, "Regulating stock buybacks."
8. Tooze, *Crashed*.
9. CoinGecko, "Global cryptocurrency market cap charts," https://www.coingecko.com/en/global-charts.
10. Taylor, "Active labour market policy in a post-Covid UK."
11. Keller & Block, "Explaining the transformation of the U.S. innovation system."
12. U.S. Department of the Treasury, "State Small Business Credit Initiative".
13. Hockett, "Finance without financiers."
14. Minsky, "The financial instability hypothesis."
15. One important example are the German public banks; Cassell, *Banking on the State*.
16. US Government Accountability Office, "DOE loan programs."
17. Lending within Islamic finance has indicated the practicality of linking long-term lending to a share in the firm's future profit stream.

7 DEMOCRATIZING HABITATION

1. In 2023, the cumulative cost was $93.1 billion; NOAA National Centers for Environmental Information (NCEI), "U.S. billion-dollar weather and climate disasters (2024)."

2. Ramirez, "Nearly 62,000 people died from record-breaking heat in Europe last summer."
3. The literature on this topic is vast, but I am drawing specifically on work on "empowered participatory governance" developed by Erik Olin Wright and Archon Fung; see Fung & Wright, *Deepening Democracy* and Wright, *Envisioning Real Utopias*.
4. Michels, *Political Parties*.
5. Baiocchi & Ganuza, *Popular Democracy*.
6. Piketty, *Capital and Ideology*.
7. Trump, for example, has distanced himself from the traditional Republican opposition to programs such as social security and Medicare. Moreover, in targeting groups such as immigrants in Trump's case or Jews in Hitler's case, there is a redistributive promise that there would be more jobs and more resources for the "true" citizens of the nation.
8. Wallace, Goldsmith-Pinkham & Schwartz, "Excess death rates for Republican and Democratic registered voters in Florida and Ohio during the Covid-19 pandemic."
9. This possibility was prefigured in the 1960s when there was some convergence between the New Left's focus on empowering people at the local level and libertarian currents on the right; Gerstle, *The Rise and Fall of the Neoliberal Order*, ch. 3.
10. Warren's proposed tax would be a 2 per cent annual levy on wealth of more than $50 million and 6 per cent on wealth of more than $1 billion. It is estimated to raise $3.75 trillion over ten years; Warren for Senate, "Ultra-millionaire tax."
11. Lindert, *Growing Public*.
12. Wright, *Envisioning Real Utopias*.
13. This is spelled out in greater detail in Block, "Financial democratization and the transition to socialism."
14. Rahman, *Democracy Against Domination*.
15. Meyers, *Working Democracies*.
16. See, for example, Isabel Ferraras's proposal for a bicameral firm, "Democratizing the corporation."
17. Block, Keller & Negoita, "Revisiting the hidden developmental state;" Keller & Block, "New levers of state power."
18. For discussion of global financial reform, see Eatwell & Taylor, *Global Finance at Risk*; Block, "Breaking with market fundamentalism"; United Nations, *Report of the Commission of Experts of the President of the United Nations General Assembly on Reforms of the International Monetary and Financial System*.
19. Baiocchi & Ganuza, *Popular Democracy*.
20. Gilman & Eisenstein, "It's like jury duty, but for getting things done."
21. Oscar Wilde allegedly said, "The trouble with socialism is that it takes up too many evenings."

References

AAPA/The Harris Poll. *The Patient Experience: Perspectives on Today's Healthcare.* The Harris Poll, 2023. https://www.aapa.org/download/113513/?tmstv=1684243672.

Abraham, K. & J. Mallatt. "Measuring human capital." *Journal of Economic Perspectives* 36:3 (2022): 103–30.

Allegretto, S. "The teacher pay penalty has hit a new high: trends in teacher wages and compensation through 2021." Economic Policy Institute, 16 August 2022. https://www.epi.org/publication/teacher-pay-penalty-2022.

American Automotive Policy Council. *State of the U.S. Automotive Industry, 2020.* https://www.americanautomakers.org/us-economic-contributions.

American Society of Civil Engineers (ASCE). "Infrastructure investment gap 2020–2029." https://infrastructurereportcard.org/resources/investment-gap-2020-2029.

Anderson, E. *Hijacked: How Neoliberalism Turned the Work Ethic Against Workers and How Workers Can Fight Back.* Cambridge: Cambridge University Press, 2023.

Baiocchi, G. & E. Ganuza. *Popular Democracy: The Paradox of Participation.* Stanford, CA: Stanford University Press, 2017.

Bell, D. *The Coming of Post-Industrial Society: A Venture in Social Forecasting.* New York: Basic Books, 1973.

Berger, S. *Making in America: From Innovation to Market.* Cambridge, MA: MIT Press, 2013.

Berk, G. & A. Saxenian. "Rethinking antitrust for the cloud era." *Politics & Society* 51:3 (2023): 409–35.

Berman, S. *The Primacy of Politics: Social Democracy and the Making of Europe's Twentieth Century.* Cambridge: Cambridge University Press, 2006.

Bhattacharya, T. (ed.). *Social Reproduction Theory: Mapping Class, Recentering Oppression.* London: Pluto, 2017.

Bipartisan Policy Center. "Childcare is a business affair." 2021 Final Report. https://bipartisanpolicy.org/download/?file=/wp-content/uploads/2021/12/Child-Care-Business-Affair-2021_Final-Report-1.pdf.

Block, F. "Swimming against the current: the rise of a hidden developmental state in the United States." *Politics & Society* 36:2 (2008): 169–206.

Block, F. "Read their lips: taxation and the right-wing agenda." In I. Martin, A. Mehrotra & M. Prasad (eds), *The New Fiscal Sociology: Taxation in Comparative and Historical Perspective*, 68–85. Cambridge: Cambridge University Press, 2009.

Block, F. *Postindustrial Possibilities*. Berkeley, CA: University of California Press, 1990.

Block, F. *Capitalism: The Future of an Illusion*. Oakland, CA: University of California Press, 2018.

Block, F. "Financial democratization and the transition to socialism." In Block & Hockett, *Democratizing Finance*, 80–118.

Block, F. "Breaking with market fundamentalism: toward domestic and global reform." In J. Shefner & P. Fernandez-Kelly (eds), *Globalization and Beyond: New Examinations of Global Power and Its Alternatives*, 210–27. University Park, PA: Pennsylvania University Press, 2011.

Block. F. & R. Hockett (eds). *Democratizing Finance: Restructuring Credit to Transform Society*. New York: Verso, 2022.

Block, F. & M. Keller. "Where do innovations come from? Transformations in the U.S. economy, 1970–2006." *Socio-Economic Review* 7:3 (2009): 459–83.

Block, F. & M. Keller (eds). *State of Innovation: The U.S. Government's Role in Technology Development*. Abingdon: Routledge, 2011.

Block, F., M. Keller & M. Negoita. "Revisiting the hidden developmental state." *Politics & Society* 52:2 (2024): 208–40.

Block, F. & M. Somers. *The Power of Market Fundamentalism: Karl Polanyi's Critique*. Cambridge, MA: Harvard University Press, 2014.

Bonvillian, W. & P. Singer. *Advanced Manufacturing: The New American Innovation Policies*. Cambridge, MA: MIT Press, 2017.

Bourdieu, P. "The forms of capital." In J. Richardson (ed.), *Handbook of Theory and Research for the Sociology of Education*, 241–58. Westport, CT: Greenwood, 1986.

Brandt, P. & J. Whitford. "Fixing network failures: the contested case of the manufacturing extension partnership." *Socio-Economic Review* 15:2 (2017): 331–57.

Braun, B. "Exit, control, and politics: structural power and corporate governance under asset manager capitalism." *Politics & Society* 50:4 (2022): 630–54.

Braverman, H. *Labor and Monopoly Capital: The Degradation of Work in the 20th Century*. New York: Monthly Review Press, 1974.

Brzezinski, Z. *Between Two Ages: America's Role in the Technetronic Era*. New York: Viking, 1970.

Bureau of Economic Analysis (BEA). "Improved estimates of the National Income and Product Accounts for 1959–95: results of the Comprehensive Revision," Survey of Current Business, Jan–Feb 1996: 1–31.

Burgin, A. *The Great Persuasion: Reinventing Free Markets Since the Depression*. Cambridge, MA: Harvard University Press, 2012.

Butler, S. & P. Germanis. "Achieving social security reform: a 'Leninist' strategy." *CATO Journal* 3:2 (1983): 547–61.

Calvert, G. & C. Niemann. *A Disrupted History: The New Left and the New Capitalism*. New York: Random House, 1971.

Cassell, M. *Banking on the State: The Political Economy of Public Savings Banks*. Newcastle upon Tyne: Agenda, 2021.

Chandler, A. *Scale and Scope: The Dynamics of Industrial Capitalism*. Cambridge, MA: Harvard University Press, 1990.

Childcare Aware of America. "The US and the high price of child care: an examination of a broken system." 2019. https://www.childcareaware.org/our-issues/research/the-us-and-the-high-price-of-child-care-2019/.

Christophers, B. *Banking Across Borders: Placing Finance in Capitalism*. Hoboken, NJ: Wiley-Blackwell, 2013.

Congressional Budget Office. "Fair-value estimates of the cost of federal credit programs in 2019," Congressional Budget Office, June 2018, https://www.cbo.gov/publication/54095.

Congressional Research Service. "A visual depiction of the shift from defined benefit (DB) to defined contribution (DC) pension plans in the private sector," 27 December 2021. https://crsreports.congress.gov/product/pdf/IF/IF12007.

Corrado, C., C. Hulten & D. Sichel. "Measuring capital and technology: an expanded framework." In C. Corrado, J. Haltiwanger & D. Sichel (eds), *Measuring Capital in the New Economy*, 11–46. Chicago, IL: University of Chicago Press, 2005.

Corrado, C., C. Hulten & D. Sichel. "Intangible capital and U.S. economic growth." *Review of Income and Wealth* 55:3 (2009): 661–85.

Cox, D. *et al*. "Public places and commercial spaces: how neighborhood amenities foster trust and connection in American communities." Survey Center on American Life, 20 October 2021. https://www.americansurveycenter.org/research/public-places-and-commercial-spaces-how-neighborhood-amenities-foster-trust-and-connection-in-american-communities/.

Crotty, J. *Keynes Against Capitalism: His Economic Case for Liberal Socialism*. Abingdon: Routledge, 2019.

Dayen, D. "Amazon continues preying on third-party sellers: another round of fees on transactions reveals what increasingly looks like a predatory scheme." *The American Prospect*, 23 August 2022. https://prospect.org/power/amazon-continues-preying-on-third-party-sellers.

Denison, E. *Accounting for Economic Growth, 1929–1969*. Washington, DC: Brookings Institution Press, 1974.

Dunlavy, C. *Small, Medium, Large: How Government Made the U.S. into a Manufacturing Powerhouse*. Cambridge: Polity, 2024.

Eatwell, J. & L. Taylor. *Global Finance at Risk: The Case for International Regulation*. New York: The New Press, 2000.

Ehrenreich, B. "The new right attack on social welfare." In F. Block *et al.* (eds), *The Mean Season: The Attack on the Welfare State*, 161–95. New York: Pantheon, 1987.

Eisner, R. *The Total Income System of Accounts*. Chicago, IL: University of Chicago Press, 1989.

Epstein, S. *Impure Science: Aids, Activism, and the Politics of Knowledge*. Berkeley, CA: University of California Press, 1996.

Esping-Anderson, G. *Three Worlds of Welfare Capitalism*. Princeton, NJ: Princeton University Press, 1990.

Esping-Anderson, G. *Social Foundations of Postindustrial Economies*. Oxford: Oxford University Press, 1999.

Ferraras, I. "Democratizing the corporation: the bicameral firm as real utopia." *Politics & Society* 51:2 (2023): 188–224.

Fisk, C. *Working Knowledge: Employee Innovation and the Rise of Corporate Intellectual Property, 1800–1930*. Chapel Hill, NC: University of North Carolina Press, 2009.

Folbre, N. "The unproductive housewife: her evolution in nineteenth-century economic thought." *Signs* 16:3 (1991): 463–84.

Folbre, N. (ed.), *For Love or Money: Care Provision in the U.S.* New York: Russell Sage, 2012.

Folbre, N. & J. Heintz. "Investment, consumption, or public good? Unpaid work and intra-family transfers in the macro-economy." *Ekonomiaz* 91:1 (2017): 103–23.

Foundational Economy Collective. *The Foundational Economy: The Infrastructure of Everyday Life*. Manchester: Manchester University Press, 2018.

Fraser, N. "Can society be commodities all the way down? Post-Polanyian reflections on capitalist crisis." *Economy and Society* 43:4 (2014): 541–58.

Fraser, N. "Crisis of care? On the social-reproductive contradictions of contemporary capitalism." In Bhattacharya, *Social Reproduction Theory*, 21–36.

Freiberger, P. & J. Swaine. *Fire in the Valley: The Making of the Personal Computer*. Berkeley, CA: Osborne, 1984.

Fung, A. & E. O. Wright (eds), *Deepening Democracy: Institutional Innovations in Empowered Participatory Governance*. London: Verso, 2003.

Garritzmann, J., S. Hausermann & B. Palier (eds), *The World Politics of Social Investment*, vols I and II. Oxford: Oxford University Press, 2022.

Gay, E. "The Midland Revolt of 1607." *Transactions of the Royal Historical Society* 18 (1904): 195–244.

Gemici, K. "Beyond the Minsky and Polanyi moments: social origins of the foreclosure crisis." *Politics & Society* 44:1 (2016): 15–43.

Gerstle, G. *The Rise and Fall of the Neoliberal Order: America and the World in the Free Market Era*. New York: Oxford University Press, 2022.

Gertner, J. *The Idea Factory: Bell Labs and the Great Age of American Innovation*. New York: Penguin, 2012.

Gilman, H. & A. Eisenstein. "It's like jury duty, but for getting things done." *Boston Globe*, 18 August 2023. https://www.bostonglobe.com/2023/08/18/opinion/citizens-assemblies/.

Goldin, C. & L. Katz. *The Race Between Education and Technology*. Cambridge, MA: Harvard University Press, 2008.

Gray, M. & S. Suri. *Ghost Work: How to Stop Silicon Valley from Building a New Global Underclass*. Boston, MA: Houghton Mifflin Harcourt, 2019.

Hacker, J. *The Great Risk Shift*. New York: Oxford University Press, 2006.

Haskel, J. & S. Westlake. *Capitalism Without Capital: The Rise of the Intangible Economy*. Princeton, NJ: Princeton University Press, 2018.

Hassett, K. "Investment." https://www.econlib.org/library/Enc/Investment.html.

Häusermann, S., J. Garritzmann & B. Palier. "The politics of social investment: a global theoretical framework." In Garritzmann, Häusermann & Palier, *The World Politics of Social Investment*, vol. I, 59–105.

Heintz, J. "Public investments and human investments: rethinking macroeconomics from a gender perspective." In D. Elson & A. Seth (eds), *Gender Equality and Inclusive Growth: Economic Policies to Achieve Sustainable Development*, 107–22. New York: UN Women, 2019.

Hemerijck, A. (ed.) *The Uses of Social Investment*. Oxford: Oxford University Press, 2017.

Hemerijck, A., S. Ronchi & I. Plavgo. "Social investment as a conceptual framework for analyzing well-being and reforms in the 21st century." *Socio-Economic Review* 21:1 (2023): 479–500.

Hendren, N. & B. Sprung-Keyser. "A unified welfare analysis of government policies." *Quarterly Journal of Economics* 135:3 (2020): 1209–318.

Hoare, Q. & G. Nowell Smith (eds). *Selections from the Prison Notebooks of Antonio Gramsci*. New York: International Publishers, 1971.

Hockett, R. "Finance without financiers." In Block & Hockett, *Democratizing Finance*, 23–79.

Hoyert, D. "Maternal morality rates in the United States 2021." National Center for Health Statistics. https://www.cdc.gov/nchs/data/hestat/maternal-mortality/2021/maternal-mortality-rates-2021.htm.

Jacobs, M. *Short-Term America: The Causes and Cures of Our Business Myopia*. Boston, MA: Harvard Business School Press, 1991.

Johns Hopkins Bloomburg School of Public Health. "Cost of clinical trials for new drug FDA approval are fraction of total tab." 24 September 2018. https://publichealth.jhu.edu/2018/cost-of-clinical-trials-for-new-drug-FDA-approval-are-fraction-of-total-tab.

Jorgenson, D. & B. Fraumeni. "The output of the education sector." In Z. Griliches (ed.), *Output Measurement in the Service Sector*, 303–41. Chicago, IL: University of Chicago Press, 1992.

Keller, M. & F. Block. "Explaining the transformation of the U.S. innovation system: the impact of a small government program." *Socio-Economic Review* 11:4 (2013): 629–56.

Keller, M & F. Block. "The new levers of state power." *Catalyst* 7:1 (2023): 9–43.

Kendrick, J. *The Formation and Stocks of Total Capital*. New York: Columbia University Press, 1976.

Kenworthy, L. *Social Democratic Capitalism*. New York: Oxford University Press, 2019.

Keynes, J. M. *The General Theory of Employment, Interest, and Money*. New York: Harcourt, Brace & World, 1964 [1936].

KFF. "KFF survey on affordability of long-term care and support service". May 2022.https://files.kff.org/attachment/Topline-KFF-Survey-on-Affordability-of-Long-Term-Care-and-Support-Service.pdf.

Kidder, T. *The Soul of a New Machine*. New York: William Morrow, 1983.

Kitschelt, H. & P. Rehm. "Polarity reversal: the socioeconomic reconfiguration of partisan support in knowledge societies." *Politics & Society* 51:4 (2023): 520–66.

Kuhn, T. *The Structure of Scientific Revolutions*. Chicago, IL: University of Chicago Press, 1962.

Kulish, N., S. Kliff & J. Siver-Greenberg. "The U.S. tried to build a new fleet of ventilators. The mission failed." *New York Times*, 29 March 2020. https://www.nytimes.com/2020/03/29/business/coronavirus-us-ventilator-shortage.html.

Landefeld, S., J. Shaunda Villones & A. Holdren. "GDP and beyond: priorities and plans." *Survey of Current Business* 100:6 (June 2020).

Landivar, L., N. Graf & G. Rayo. "Childcare prices in local areas." U.S. Department of Labor, Women's Bureau, Issue Brief (2023). https://www.dol.gov/sites/dolgov/files/WB/NDCP/WB_IssueBrief-NDCP-final.pdf.

Lester, R. & M. Piore. *Innovation: The Missing Dimension*. Cambridge, MA: Harvard University Press, 2004.

Lindert, P. *Growing Public: Social Spending and Economic Growth Since the Eighteenth Century*. Cambridge: Cambridge University Press, 2004.

Mazzucato, M. *The Entrepreneurial State*. New York: Anthem, 2013.

Mazzucato, M. *The Value of Everything: Making and Taking in the Global Economy*. New York: Public Affairs, 2018.

McDonough, W. & M. Braungart. *Cradle to Cradle: Remaking the Way we Make Things*. New York: North Point Press, 2002.

McGee, H. *The Sum of Us: What Racism Costs Everyone and How We Can Prosper Together*. New York: One World, 2021.

McMichael, C. "3 next-gen helmet designs that could curb concussions in the NFL." Digital Trends, 16 February 2022. https://www.digitaltrends.com/news/nfl-helmet-challenge-winners-technology/.

Meyers, J. *Working Democracies: Managing Inequality in Worker Cooperatives*. Ithaca, NY: Cornell University Press, 2022.

Michels, R. *Political Parties: A Sociological Study of the Oligarchic Tendencies of Modern Democracy*. New York: The Free Press, 1962 [1911].

Minsky, H. "The financial instability hypothesis: an interpretation of Keynes and an alternative to 'standard' theory." *Challenge* 20:1 (1977): 20–27.

Mirowski, P. & D. Plehwe (eds). *The Road from Mont Pelerin: The Making of the Neoliberal Thought Collective*. Cambridge, MA: Harvard University Press, 2009.

Mizruchi, M. *The Fracturing of the American Corporate Elite*. Cambridge, MA: Harvard University Press, 2013.

Molotch, H. "The city as a growth machine: toward a political economy of place". *American Journal of Sociology* 82:2 (1976): 309–32.

Morning Consult. "State of childcare in the United States." June 2023. https://production-tcf.imgix.net/app/uploads/2023/06/20210511/TCF_Childcare_Jun23.pdf.

Morel, N., B. Palier & J. Palme (eds). *Towards a Social Investment Welfare State? Ideas, Policies, Challenges*. Bristol: Policy Press, 2012.

Mudge, S. *Leftism Reinvented: Western Parties from Socialism to Neoliberalism*. Cambridge, MA: Harvard University Press, 2018.

Muro, M. & S. Liu. "As the digitalization of work expands, place-based solutions can bridge the gaps". Brookings Metro, 7 February 2023. https://www.brookings.edu/articles/as-the-digitalization-of-work-expands-place-based-solutions-can-bridge-the-gaps/.

National Research Council. *Funding a Revolution: Government Support for Computing Research*. Washington, DC: The National Academies Press, 1999.

Newfield, C. *The Great Mistake: How We Wrecked Public Universities and How We can Fix Them*. Baltimore, MD: Johns Hopkins University Press, 2016.

NOAA National Centers for Environmental Information (NCEI). "U.S.

billion-dollar weather and climate disasters (2024)." https://www.ncei.noaa.gov/access/billions/.

OECD Family Database. "Public spending on family benefits." Updated February 2023. https://www.oecd.org/els/soc/PF1_1_Public_spending_on_family_benefits.pdf.

Palladino, L. & W. Lazonick. "Regulating stock buybacks: the $6.3 trillion dollar question." *International Review of Applied Economics* 38:1–2 (2022): 243–67.

Parker, R. & B. Grimm. "Recognition of business and government expenditures for software as investment: methodology and quantitative impacts, 1959–1998." Bureau of Economic Analysis, 2000. https://www.bea.gov/research/papers/2000/recognition-business-and-government-expenditures-software-investment.

Pew Research Center. "Inflation, health costs, partisan cooperation among the nation's top problems." 21 June 2023. https://www.pewresearch.org/politics/2023/06/21/inflation-health-costs-partisan-cooperation-among-the-nations-top-problems/.

Piketty, T. *Capital in the Twenty-First Century*. Trans. A. Goldhammer. Cambridge, MA: Harvard University Press, 2014.

Piketty, T. *Capital and Ideology*. Trans. A. Goldhammer. Cambridge, MA: Harvard University Press, 2020.

Polanyi, K. *The Great Transformation: The Political and Economic Origins of Our Time*. Boston, MA: Beacon Press, 2001 [1944].

Polanyi, K. "The economy as instituted process." In G. Dalton (ed.), *Primitive, Archaic, and Modern Economies*. Boston, MA: Beacon Press, 1968.

Putnam, R. *Bowling Alone: The Collapse and Revival of American Community*. New York: Simon & Schuster, 2001.

Rabinowitz, B. *Defensive Nationalism: Explaining the Rise of Populism and Fascism in the 21st Century*. New York: Oxford University Press, 2023.

Rama, A. "National health expenditures, 2018: spending growth remains steady even with increases in private health insurance and Medicare spending." Policy Research Perspectives, American Medical Association. https://www.ama-assn.org/system/files/2020-08/prp-annual-spending-2018.pdf.

Ramirez, R. "Nearly 62,000 people died from record-breaking heat in Europe last summer. It's a lesson for the US, too." CNN, 14 July 2023. https://www.cnn.com/2023/07/10/world/deadly-europe-heatwave-2022-climate/index.html.

Rich, A. *Think Tanks, Public Policy and the Politics of Expertise*. Cambridge: Cambridge University Press, 2004.

Sabeel Rahman, K. *Democracy Against Domination*. New York: Oxford University Press, 2017.

Schrank, A. & J. Whitford. "The anatomy of network failure." *Sociological Theory* 29:3 (2011): 151–77.

Schultz, T. "Investment in human capital." *American Economic Review* 51:1 (1961): 1–17.

Schumpeter, J. *Capitalism, Socialism and Democracy*. Third edn. New York: Harper, 1962 [1942].

Slobodian, Q. *Globalists: The End of Empire and the Birth of Neoliberalism*. Cambridge, MA: Harvard University Press, 2018.

Smarth Growth America/Hattaway Communications, *American Attitudes on Transportation Spending*. Survey Findings Report. https://smartgrowthamerica.org/wp-content/uploads/2023/07/FINAL-June-2023-Full-Survey-Data-for-release-1.pdf.

Smith, A. *The Theory of Moral Sentiments*. Ed. K. Haakonssen. Cambridge: Cambridge University Press, 2002 [1759].

Smith, A. *The Wealth of Nations*. Ed. E. Cannan. Chicago, IL: University of Chicago Press, 1976 [1776].

Smith, D. & R. Alexander. *Fumbling the Future: How Xerox Invented, Then Ignored, the First Personal Computer*. New York: Morrow, 1988.

Soloveichik, R. & D. Wasshausen. "Copyright-protected assets in the National Accounts." Bureau of Economic Analysis, 2013. https://www.bea.gov/research/papers/2013/copyright-protected-assets-national-accounts.

Solow, R. "Technical change and the aggregate production function." *Review of Economics and Statistics* 39:3 (1957): 312–20.

Suh, J. & N. Folbre. "Valuing unpaid child care in the U.S.: a prototype satellite account using the American time use survey." *Review of Income and Wealth* 62: 4 (2015): 668–84.

Taylor, A. "Active labour market policy in a post-Covid UK: moving beyond a 'work first' approach." City-REDI blog, University of Birmingham. https://blog.bham.ac.uk/cityredi/active-labour-market-policy-in-a-post-covid-uk-moving-beyond-a-work-first-approach/.

Toffler, A. *Future Shock*. New York: Random House, 1970.

Tooze, A. *Crashed: How a Decade of Financial Crises Changed the World*. New York: Viking, 2018.

Toupin, L. *Wages for Housework: A History of an International Feminist Movement, 1972–1977*. Vancouver, BC: University of British Columbia Press, 2018.

Touraine, A. *The Post-Industrial Society*. Trans. L. Mayhew. New York: Random House, 1971.

Tyson, A., C. Funk & B. Kennedy. "What the data says about Americans' views of climate change." Pew Research Center, 9 August 2023. https://www.pewresearch.org/short-reads/2023/08/09/what-the-data-says-about-americans-views-of-climate-change/.

United Nations. Report of the Commission of Experts of the President of the United Nations General Assembly on Reforms of the International Monetary and Financial System, 21 September 2009. https://www.un.org/en/ga/econcrisissummit/docs/FinalReport_CoE.pdf.

US Government Accountability Office. "DOE loan programs." GAO-15-438, 27 April 2015. https://www.gao.gov/products/gao-15-438.

U.S. Department of the Treasury. "State Small Business Credit Initiative." Fact sheet June 2023. https://home.treasury.gov/system/files/256/State-Small-Business-Credit-Initiative-SSBCI-Fact-Sheet.pdf.

Vogel, L. *Marxism and the Oppression of Women: Toward a Unitary Theory*. New Brunswick, NJ: Rutgers University Press, 1983.

Wallace, J., P. Goldsmith-Pinkham & J. Schwartz. "Excess death rates for Republican and Democratic registered voters in Florida and Ohio during the Covid-19 pandemic." *JAMA Internal Medicine* 183:9 (2023): 916–23.

Warren for Senate. "Ultra-millionaire tax." https://elizabethwarren.com/plans/ultra-millionaire-tax.

Whitford, J. & A. Schrank. "The paradox of the weak state revisited: industrial policy, network governance, and political decentralization." In F. Block & M. Keller (eds), *State of Innovation: The U.S. Government's Role in Technology Development*, 261–81. Boulder, CO: Paradigm, 2011.

Womack, J., D. Jones & D. Roos. *The Machine that Changed the World: The Story of Lean Production*. New York: HarperCollins, 1991.

Wright, E. O. *Envisioning Real Utopias*. New York: Verso, 2010.

Index

Page numbers with an "n" denote notes; numbers in **bold** denote figures.

agriculture 16, 22, 23, 65, 92, 147
Antitrust legislation 13
austerity 93, 117, 118
autocrats 8, 159
automotive industry 4, 14–15, 41, 51, 55, 76, 84, 87
automation 37, 52, 76

banks/banking 18, 47, 67, 77, 126–7, 129–32, 133–5, 150 *see* community banks
   Dodd-Frank bill (2010) 131
   Landesbanken 134
Bell, Daniel 6, 37, 44
Bell Labs 40, 68–9
Biden, Joe 128–9, 132, 145, 153
Big Pharma 39, 41, 48, 77–9, 85
billionaire class 8, 89, 134, 148, 159
blocked transition 2, 6–7
Bureau of Economic Analysis (BEA) 92, 94, 96, 97, 102–103, 107–108, 110, 112–13, 148

capital 68, 95, 96, 104, 121, 126
   consumption 94
   cultural 95
   flight 149, 150
   investments 115, 129, 133
   intangible 115–16
   scarcity 130–31
   startup 127–8, 150
   strike 149

care economy 33, 145, 156
childcare 29, 31, 33, 100, 101–102, 104, 106, 110–12
China 22, 83–4, 95, 154–5
citizens' assemblies 19, 62, 133, 140–41, 157
climate change 11, 26, 27, 31, 34, 124, 128, 137–9, 141, 154–5
collaborative/cooperative network production 14–15, 41–2, 76–9, 80, 82, 85, 86, 88, 89, 133–5
   third-party role 73–5
collateralized mortgage obligation (CMO) bonds 123
commodities, standardized/classical 12–14, 28–9, 47–9, 51
communications 39, 40, 43, 56–7
community banks 131–3
community development financial institutions (CDFI) 131–2
computerization 37–8, 39, 68
consumption
   capital 94–5
   household spending 95–6
   mass 3, 9
   personal expenditure 16, 49, **50**, 51, 105
   shared 62–3
   subscription model 54–6
   tax 149
corporations
   as business organizations 65–6

consolidation 67
executive pay 122
finance of 18, 67–8
market power 14–15
and pensions 18
self-financing 124, 130, 148
share buybacks 18
structure 41, 66, 81, 84–6, 87, 91
workforce skills 82
corporate laboratories 69, 70
Covid-19 21, 32, 62, 81, 83, 88, 128, 144, 153, 155
credit unions 131–3
crime 29, 34, 59, 140, 159
cryptocurrencies 123, 127, 163–4n3

Dalla Costa, M. 100
Defense Advanced Research Projects Agency (DARPA) 43, 75
deindustrialization 25, 37
democratic governance, local 1, 139–43, 156–7
depreciation 58, 94, 95, 109, 114–15, 165n7, 167n51
derivatives 123–4, 148
Dunlavy, C. 163n3

economics
  mainstream 6–7, 12, 14, 16
  failure of categories 7, 27–8, 31, 45, 48, 49, 91–2, 96, 117–18
  measurement of investment 92
  trickle down 129–30
economy
  drivers of 17
  formal v substantive (Polanyi) 28, 47
  global economy, reform of 142, 153–5
  knowledge economy 35, 101
  and the individual 5–6
  innovation economy 21–22, 38, 68
  investment 91–2
  market economy 47
  shift to a service economy 6, 10, 94
education
  levels of 2, 44
  higher 9, 30, 35, 44–5, 51, 77, 119, 126
  charter schools 63
  and training 97–8, 102, 104, 105, 110

secondary 119–20
Ehrenreich, B. 165-6n28
employee empowerment 151–2
enclosures 24–5
energy, clean 26, 34, 42, 118, 128–9, 131, 135, 138, 155
entrepreneurs 41, 68, 78, 79, 95, 126–7, 147
entertainment industry 38, 55, 56–7, 76
environmentalism 11, 12, 31, 34
Esping-Andersen, G. 101–02
everyday libertarianism 5

Federici, S. 100
feminist critique *see* social reproduction
fictitious commodities (Polanyi) 47, 163n1
finance 17–18, 119–36
  alternative sources/system 129, 130–32, 133–5
  bonds 121–3
  clinical trials 78
  corporate 67–8
  to support cooperative network production 134–5
  financial capital 121
  and housing 59, 125
  and infrastructure 125–6
  and vocational skills 126
  and start ups 126–7
  and green agenda 128–9
  and banks 130
financial instruments 39
financialization 8, 121
Ford, Henry 51, 76
foundational economy 161n1
free markets 6, 19, 23, 122
  theorists, 35–6, 45
Friedman, M. 6, 35, 36

Germany 44, 113, 152
gross domestic product (GDP) 7, 31, 91–2, 93, 97, 99, 110, 113, 148–9
gig economy 82–3
global financial crisis (2008–09) 36, 45, 123, 153, 155
Gramsci, A. 1, 2, 3, 4
guesstimates, use of 107

overseas cheap labour 22, 52, 76, 82, 83
Owen, R. 8

participatory democracy 19–20, 139
pensions 17, 18
Physiocrats, the 92, 99
Piketty, T. 2, 95, 143
Polanyi, K. 23, 24, 25, 26, 28, 47, 161n2, 162n5
politics
  citizen participation 11, 19, 63, 140–41, 157
  polarization of 144–5
postindustrial society 4, 6 *see* habitation
price mechanism 45, 48–9
  theorists 35–7, 101
production, mass 14, 25, 31, 39, 49, 52, 65, 71, 75–6, 80, 83, 84, 87, 97, 99, 109, 114, 153 *see also* collaborative network production
public goods 75, 125
public research centres 15, 43, 69, 70
publicly funded research 43–4, 70
race/racism 10, 12, 60, 63
Reagan, R. 35, 36, 117, 119, 122
Ricardo, D. 47, 117
role of government spending 6, 11, 13, 15, 17, 34, 35–7, 40–44, 48, **108**, 109, **110**, **113**, 117, 118, **144**, 147, 149, 150, 153
  bank bailout 131
  in healthcare 60–61
  in housing 58–60, 125
  limits on effectiveness 58–62
  in research 70, 71
  in transportation 61–2
  rural areas 34, 146–7
Schrank, A. 73
Schultz, T. 97
Schumpeter, J. 26
second-hand markets 39
self interest 32
service sector 12, 13, 23, 35, 53, 65
share buybacks 18, 122–3
Silicon Valley 84, 88

skills, employee 97, 98, 100, 102, 104–05, 116, 126, 165n7
Small Business Administration 18, 127–8
Small Business Innovation Research (SBIR) program 43, 74, 127
Smith, A. 47, 162n8
social reproduction 22, 31, 93, 99–101, 102, **110**, 113 *see also* housework; unpaid work
  and social investment 99–101
  Marxist theory of 100–101
  elements of investment 106–07
  new framework for 102, 105–07
social security benefits 111, 122
social welfare spending 93, 101
Solow, R. 96
specialized expertise 15, 70, 76, 134
subscription model of consumption 14, 54–6, 58
taxation/tax revenues 103, 109, 117, 119, 120, 141, 148–9
  global transaction tax 155
VAT 149
Taylorism 80–83
tech firms 39, 84–7, 88, 118, 126–7
technology, advances 6, 22, 26, 27, 38, 52, 68, 87, 97, 135, 137
technocrats 11, 62
Thatcher, M. 35, 36, 163n5
traffic congestion/pollution 34
transportation 26, 61–2
personal expenditure **50**
trickle-down economics 129
Trump, D. 1, 57, 144, 145, 146, 168n7
unionization 25, 152
unpaid work 22, 100, **110** *see also* housework; social reproduction
US national income accounts *see* national income accounts, Bureau of Economic Analysis (BEA)
wage demands 117
well-being 30, 143, 158
Whitford, J. 73
World Bank 142, 154
Wright, E. O. 150

INDEX

habitation 21-46
choice of term 21
democratizing 16, 19-20, 137-44
economy v society 4, 9
improvement of 24, 26-7
and Polanyi 23-6
as synthesis of critiques 31-2
public conceptions of 33-4
society 10-12, 14
value of concept 28-9, 30
and work 21-2
Hausermann, S. 102
Hayek, F. 35, 36
healthcare 12, 26, 29, 33, 48, 54, 60-61, 62, 77, 84, 104, 112, 157
Obama reforms 63
personal expenditure on 50
Hockett, R. 130
housework 99, 100, 104 *see* social reproduction
housing 10, 29, 33, 45-6, 52, 54, 58-60, 62, 63, 125, 146
personal expenditure on 50
human capital 95, 97, 98, 100, 102
income
household 30
inequality 8, 18, 32, 62, 77, 122, 143
and personal expenditure 50
support 104, 110, 111
Indigenous peoples 25, 31-2
inequality 2, 8, 18, 62, 77, 135, 143, 157
Inflation Reduction Act (IRA) 70, 129, 132, 153
infrastructure projects 10-11, 43, 61-2, 117, 120, 133, 138
funding 125-6
innovation 14, 15, 39, 68, 69, 74, 75-7, 79, 82, 85-6, 88, 102, 134, 148
role of government 40-43
football helmet case study 71-3
intangible investments 97, 114, 115, 116, 165n23
intellectual property 13, 39, 42, 73, 74, 81-2, 84, 97
International Monetary Fund 154-5
internet 27, 36, 52, 57
internet platform firms 27, 38, 66, 69, 79-80, 85

James, S. 100
Japan 87

Keynes, J. M. 3, 95, 96, 109-10, 113, 154
Kuhn, T. 92, 99

loan guarantee schemes 18

manufacturing 3, 37, 76, 134
employment 22-3, 44, 82
Manufacturing Extension Program (MEP) 74
Marxism 99, 101
mass customization 3, 9, 13, 39, 52
McGhee, H. 63
Michels, R. 139
Mittelstand 134
monoculture 65, 66, 68, 73
morbid symptoms 1-2, 4
municipal bonds 120

national income accounts/accounting 92-6, 103, 117 *see also* Bureau of Economic Analysis (BEA)
neoliberalism 6, 23, 153
New Deal 3, 145
NFL 71-3
non-profits 41, 42, 80, 103, 106, 108, 112, 113, 126-8, 150, 166n35
financing agencies 131, 132-3, 134
Nordic countries 102

OECD 9, 111, 112, 114, 148
outsourcing 76

dot-com bubble 123, 131
investment 91-118
business investment 17, 91, 110
and conceptions of capital 95
depreciation 114-15
economic accounting 16
government investment 43, 108, 110
gross versus net 94, 114
measurement of 16-17, 92-3, 93-8, 117
new definition of 102-03
new measurement of 103-05, 107-08, 110-13, 113
sources of 108

181